Robert Robertson

in the countries of the mind

Copyright © 2018 Robert Robertson

All rights reserved.

ISBN:1985567520
ISBN-13:9781985567528

TO CLAUDETTE

without your help and support this book would have been impossible

also by Robert Robertson
(with dates of first performances, first screenings, publication)

Operas
The Kingdom (1984)
The Cathars (1995)
Empedocles (music/film version of dance opera *Empedocles*, film by Dennis Dracup, 1995)

Plays
Chichikov (1981)
Rabelaisdada (1993)

Music/Films
Oserake and The River That Walks (2002)
Invisible City (in progress)
Victoria Tenebrae (2015)
Edge of Chaos (2016)
Diversions: Machines, Cityzens, River (2017)

Films
I'm Back (2007)
Assault on Time (2008)
Trace Elements (2008)

Books
Eisenstein on the Audiovisual (2009, 2011)
Awarded the Kraszna-Krausz Prize, 2010
Rabelaisdada (2014), illustrated by Ebenezer Splodge
Cinema and the Audiovisual Imagination (2015)

Website
https://www.ocatilloaudiovisual.com

...consider all the extensive regions that lie open behind you, and all the peoples in them: you will never find an area forbidden to you so large that an even larger one is not left open.

Seneca, *On Tranquillity of Mind*

scattering texts

1. in the countries of the mind

contents

preface xi
note xiii
1. glass thinking   xiv
2. arty   1
3. joyous faces   1
4. rhythm   1
5. when it's useful to be unknown   1
6. archival connections   2
7. Manhattan morning   3
8. Empedocles in Oxford   3
9. time, perception   4
10. inspiring rehearsal   4
11. *River* from *Diversions*   5
12. art in the present   5
13. legislators   5
14. our brains   6
15. a leap, a dip   6
16. a pun   6
17. Tolstoy's confession   7
18. American Abstract Expressionists   7
19. Joyeux party!   8
20. The Glass Bead Game   9
21. Havana morning   11
22. failed pictures   12
23. theorism   12
24. spatial/temporal orientation   12
25. glass mask   14
26. *Breaking the Frame*   15
27. Nimrud, etc   16
28. *Working from Ignorance*   17
29. a unique gallery   36
30. the sales pitch   37
31. perceptions   38

32. *The Drunken Boat*   38
33. emotions   38
34. *Dad's Army*   39
35. mapping the brain   39
36. prize   40
37. Montreal snow   40
38. not illustrations   41
39. different countries   41
40. after hours   41
41. deciphering ancient manuscripts   42
42. the kye-nee-ma   44
43. what's this?   47
44. time and memory   47
45. immigration   48
46. a glittering line   48
47. I am   49
48. night, fog   49
49. remote interactions   49
50. a secret   50
51. door of the spirits   51
52. what everyone likes   51
53. Minsk: a joint adventure   52
54. hubs   56
55. aspects of education   56
56. the algorithmic society   57
57. multiple approaches   59
58. objects on a shelf   59
59. collective opinion   59
60. a story from World War I   60
61. significant funerals   60
62. intellectuals   60
63. melting into air – a letter from my grandfather   61
64. an extraordinary masterclass   62
65. what is rhythm?   63
66. ice on hotel, Montreal   63

67. the unknown   *64*
68. empty   *64*
69. open/close   *64*
70. writers   *65*
71. migration   *65*
72. frontiers   *65*
73. night trees   *66*
74. illusion, or not an illusion?   *66*
75. urban sun   *67*
76. the artist as enemy   *67*
77. no style   *67*
78. unpredictability   *68*
79. chaos   *68*
80. crossing   *69*
81. the dog leaps   *70*
82. unpredictable   *70*
83. authority   *71*
84. labels   *71*
85. the container   *72*
86. vertical/horizontal   *72*
87. the crocodile and the hen   *73*
88. America   *74*
89. *The Virginity of Place*   *75*
90. to explore   *87*
91. Manhattan morning   *87*
92. hyper-diffractive thinking   *88*
93. a music/film about a city in winter   *89*
94. the point of view   *90*
95. Cap-Haïtien, 14th August   *90*
96. MIND YOUR HEAD   *94*
97. monstrous things   *95*
98. worktable, Montreal   *96*
99. non-linear narratives   *96*

100. chance *97*
101. the secret of a jockey's Grand National success *97*
102. inspiring Hockney retrospective *97*
103. at a time *99*
104. a village near St Petersburg *99*
105. acceptance, rejection *99*
106. a different approach *100*
107. brands hatch *100*
108. waiting *100*
109. influence *101*
110. the highest *101*
111. first arrival in Moscow *102*
112. unpredictable art *102*
113. the Jarman Building *103*
114. perfection *103*
115. identity crisis *104*
116. foreign *104*
117. *Ways of Knowing* *105*
118. *Diversions* *121*
119. illusions of illusions *121*
120. London rain *121*
121. *Machines* *122*
122. money *122*
123. multi-phonic *Rabelaisdada* *123*
124. iridescent mind *123*
125. light and sound *123*
126. audiovisual montage *124*
127. *Rabelaisdada*, a satire *125*
128. an American space *129*
129. making places *130*
130. Manhattan morning *132*
origins *133*
131. reflections *153*

x

preface

On this planet there are countries which are open,

and others which are closed.

The same principle applies (and there is a continual fight)

in the countries of the mind.

note

This non-linear book is in the form of a small exhibition.

The texts and images are numbered,

but these numbers are in a chance-derived order.

This way, the reader can follow any order they like.

In exhibitions you can find yourself looking at a label by the painting,

before looking at the painting itself.

This is why I have attributed the texts in the back of this

little exhibition book, under *origins*.

Some texts may have opposite points of view – why not?
This is what happens in life.

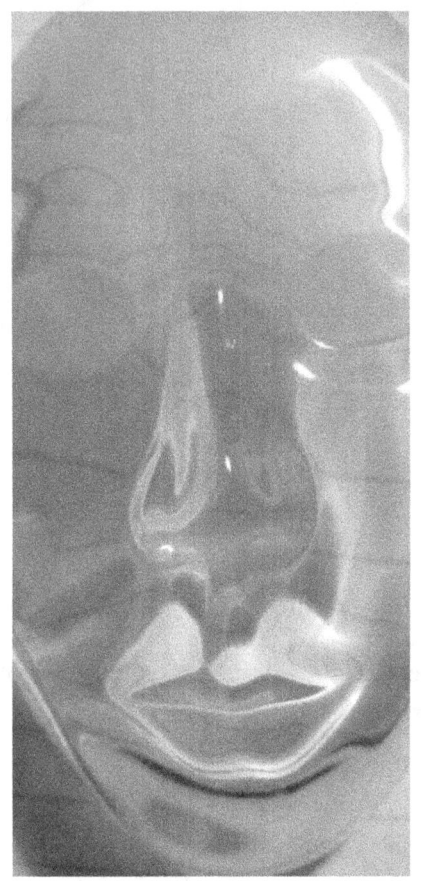

1. glass thinking

2. arty

Arty is not arty is not art.

3. joyous faces
Amused by big images of illustrious alumni
displayed on the windows of a venerable academic institution -
most of their faces are tired-looking and glum,
in stark contrast with the photos that are displayed next to them,
of the faces of youthful students,
each one radiating a perfect smile.

4. rhythm
In art you fight continuously against the inertia of the known.

This is where rhythm comes from –
all exciting art works at the edge of incoherence.

5. when it's useful to be unknown

A boat hired by the Greek Ministry of Culture, full of Greek poets, so they could meet publishers.

A well-known publisher from London was there.

On the boat he was besieged by poets, trapped.

Meanwhile, unknown, I was left completely alone.

I stood outside on the deck and watched the slow curves of Athena lying down - the shapes of the Peloponnese coastline passing by.

Being surprised by the scent of the sun-warmed pistachio trees, across the water, approaching the island of Aegina in a small boat.

Exploring Hydra with its desolate rockiness, on my own.

Just contemplating the sea, empty of boats, with its games of light on the water, and shadows.

6. archival connections

On a business trip to Havana I had some time to spare, so I thought I'd pop in to visit the Alejo Carpentier Foundation.

There I met his widow, Lilia Andrea Esteban de Carpentier.

In the Foundation's library she showed me copies of the reviews of my first opera *The Kingdom*.

(I'd based my libretto on her husband's novel *The Kingdom of This World*).

This meeting in Havana took place fourteen years after the première of *The Kingdom* in Amsterdam.

Now twenty years after my visit to the Carpentier Foundation, *Eisenstein on the Audiovisual* is being used internationally for courses on the audiovisual in cinema, by film specialists who won't know that I used Eisenstein's montage of attractions method to structure *The Kingdom*.

Over thirty years after the first production of *The Kingdom*, a three-camera video of the work, along with the music and related production materials is now in the Special Collections section of the library at the University of Amsterdam.

It's like when we travel at 30,000 feet for thousands of miles:

we have very little idea of what's happened or is happening below,

just as when we're on the ground, we don't know who is flying up there, thousands of feet above us.

And we also don't know what's happening in most places we have never visited,

let alone if they are thousands of miles away.

As this applies to people, so it applies to ideas.

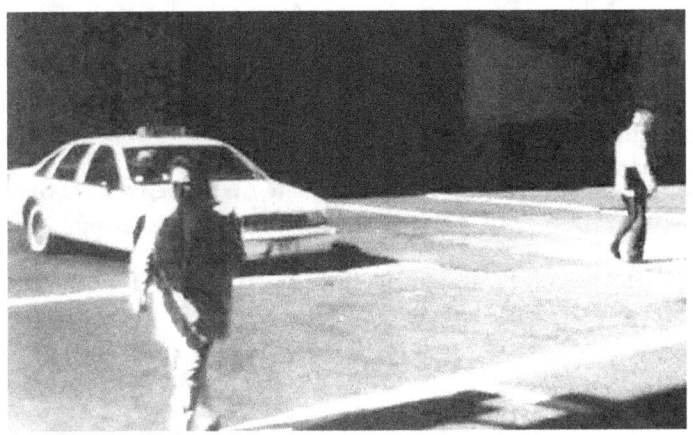

7. Manhattan morning

8. Empedocles in Oxford

    The audience for the screening of the music/film *Empedocles* on the evening of the 3rd July, was varied and multi-disciplinary in the Oxford University tradition: students, emeritus professors, specialists on Empedocles and the philosophy of ancient Greece. Dr Anna Marmodoro, Fellow in Philosophy at Corpus Christi College, organised this event to start her international conference on the philosopher Empedocles.
The artist and filmmaker Dennis Dracup and I introduced the work, suitably accompanied by excellent Italian wine.
The audience was enthusiastic.
Not for them the fatuous focus on contemporary style wars,
the current equivalents of the 18th century French versus Italian opera 'wars', later: Brahms against Wagner,
later: Schoenberg against Stravinsky.
The further back you look through your temporal telescope,
the more laughable these conflicts become.
However, these 'wars' do provide a living for professional critics, who foster such labels to encourage simplistic oppositions and battles for supremacy.

9. time, perception

How does time relate to our perception of the visual world?

How does time relate to our perception of music?

And how does our perception of time relate to our perception of the visual world?

And our perception of music relate to our perception of time?

10. inspiring rehearsal

We went to an inspiring rehearsal of Beethoven's *Violin Concerto in D Major*, at the Royal College of Music, with not one, but three excellent violinists, one for each movement, and one who played a Stradivarius violin made in 1728.

The Amaryllis Fleming Concert Hall has an excellent acoustic, and the playing, as is often the case with top student orchestras, was full of passion, energy, vigour, and total commitment.

The conductor, Mark Messenger, concentrated on precision in the rhythmic details, and made intriguing points (as for example how Beethoven's silences are very different from Mozart's silences), and generally he strongly emphasised the improvisatory qualities of Beethoven's only violin concerto.

(This reminded me how years ago a filmmaker had asked me, as a composer, what I thought of improvisation. I told him that for me, the best notated music should sound like the best improvisation imaginable).

I particularly enjoy rehearsals like this one, as in them you experience the actual progress of composition of the music, its separate parts, its assemblage. In this rehearsal we were vividly reminded of Beethoven's extensive range of orchestral colours in this concerto, his melodic vivacity, harmonic daring, rhythmic force: all the inner workings of inspired music, and music-making.

11. *River*, from *Diversions*

River is about association and perception,
movement and reflection.

12. art in the present

To me there is no past or future in art.
If a work of art cannot live always in the present it must not be considered at all.
The art of the Greeks, of the Egyptians, of the great painters who lived in other times,
is not an art of the past;
perhaps it is more alive today than it ever was.

13. legislators

Primo Levi wrote that 'the legislator of poetry is not the poet but the grammarian'.

The legislator of music is not the composer, but the musicologist.

Something similar could be said about any creative activity.

But what about those artists who were also theorists?

Rameau, Eisenstein, da Vinci?

Yes, they theorised, but they weren't just describing, they were exploring.

And this is why art schools and music schools shouldn't really be part of universities –

as they could become legislators of ideas.

14. our brains

Our brains are layers of multiple years.

15. a leap, a dip

'The tiger leapt, and the swallow dipped her wings in dark pools on the other side of the world'

16. a pun

Years ago, when I was at a Film Studies seminar in Montreal,
I couldn't help noticing that the doctoral students kept repeating the word 'coded' whenever a still from a film was being analysed:
'Oh, that (object) there is *coded*, and that (object) over there is *coded*'
and so on, and so on.
In exasperation I raised my hand, 'coated in *what?*' I asked.
A mixture of consternation and laughter ensued.
Nobody could answer my question,
but from then onwards,
coded/coated objects as if by magic
had disappeared.

17. Tolstoy's confession

Tolstoy isn't immediately associated with a sense of humour,

and it's not there very much in his relatively short text *A Confession*.

At one point he makes a wonderfully astute comment on ignorance:

'when it does not know something it says that the thing it does not know is stupid.'

Due to censorship, *A Confession* couldn't be published in Tolstoy's lifetime,

and the same fate was shared by his text *What is Art?*

In part of this text he writes a hilarious account of a production of Wagner's opera *Siegfried*.

Check it out!

18. American Abstract Expressionists

Exhilarating show at London's Royal Academy. Was struck by two main things in this work: the lack of compromise, and the extraordinary energy of these artists.

Also, this work is very musical. Motherwell's unique *Plato's Cave* was there – I remembered how it had inspired me for certain sections in the *Machines* orchestral piece.

However I did miss Motherwell's *Open* series, especially the huge bright red colour field paintings, which were one of the inspirations for *River*, the orchestral movement I'd originally placed after *Machines*.

Afterwards, I drove round the area around de Kooning's studio, and also the Jackson Pollock-Lee Krasner studio in Springs, Long Island. Very impressed by the light there, in both winter and summer: you just drive along, and the summer greenery suddenly becomes a gentle beige with a light covering of snow, instantly. I've never had time to actually visit this part of Long Island - when passing through Penn Station I'd always wanted to hop on a train to go there.

Now on the computer screen I see that there's no high street in Springs, just isolated houses, which reminded me of my visit to meet the choreographer Martha Clarke, who lives in the house formerly owned by Arshile Gorky in Connecticut, set in a very different, hilly landscape. He installed a huge glazed wall at one end of it, for his studio. The house is surrounded by a very fertile wilderness, which surges through in his paintings.

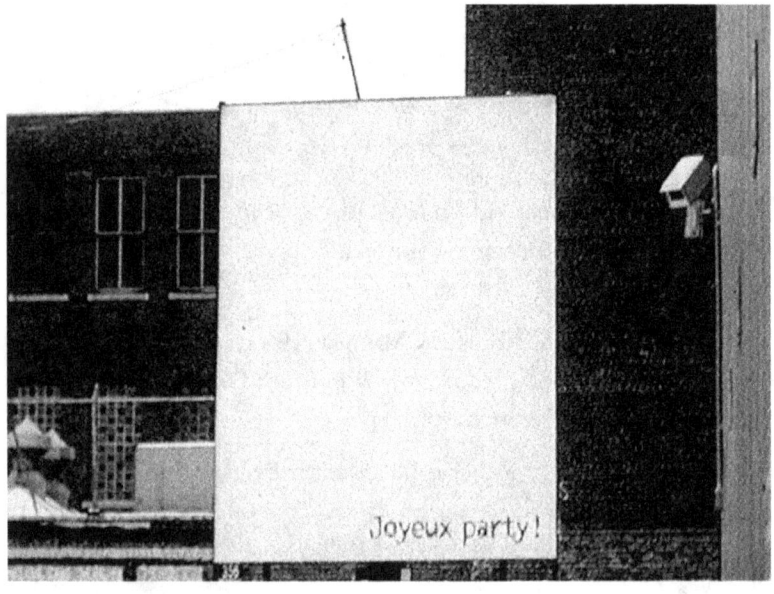

19. Joyeux party!

20. The Glass Bead Game

Magically, it happens that a book will draw your attention to it, almost as if it's saying to you: *I'm here, lost among all your other books - you should read me now!*

This is what happened to me recently when I noticed a copy of *The Glass Bead Game* by Hermann Hesse, which drew attention to itself, calling out to me from the book shelves.

It brought to mind something which had happened a few years ago: an immediate response from a Professor Emerita, after a screening of *Empedocles*, the music/film realisation of my dance opera about the life and ideas of the Early Greek philosopher Empedocles. The music/film version of this work was made in collaboration with the artist filmmaker Dennis Dracup, who used his 'choreography of light' concept in the film, on the pre-existing recording of my music.

This particular screening of *Empedocles* had opened a conference on the philosopher, which was held at the Ioannou Centre for Classical and Byzantine Studies at Oxford University. After the screening, Professor Eva Wagner had leapt up to me, beaming and enthusiastically exclaiming 'the Glass Bead Game!'. Delighted, I thanked her, and made a note to look up Hermann Hesse's novel.

Now more than four years later, I think that I know what she meant: in effect the bringing together and off-setting of the philosophical ideas with the visual contents, in a continuous audiovisual counterpoint with the music of the dance opera. A form of unity, a synthesis of what would otherwise be completely disparate musical, visual, poetic and philosophical ideas – in other words a work analogous to those made through the Glass Bead Game.

To emphasise the musical and transformational nature of the Game, Hesse quotes Novalis: 'in eternal transmutations the secret power of song greets us here below'.

Hesse tells us that the Game uses music. Associated from the earliest times with a magical power to encourage in a group of people the same mood, music brings together the rhythm of their heartbeats and their breathing. And he emphasises what he calls 'the improvisatory agility of the Game's language'.

Hesse describes how, as the Game developed, it became separated into different disciplines, and a puritanical wariness of digressions encouraged these separations to remain in force. However, in time, due to the changing dominance of these disciplines, they had progressively come together in the form of a multi-disciplinary language in which values could be expressed and compared.

Though the Game was first and foremost 'a form of music-making', Hesse mentions how it could start from sources as varied as a configuration of celestial bodies, a statement from Leibniz or the Upanishads, a theme from a fugue by J.S. Bach. These elements would be explored and developed, compared to similar ideas, so that for example, a piece of classical music could be compared to a formula found in the laws of nature.

By using ideas and themes in counterpoint with each other, a synthesis could be derived from opposites.

This synthesis is one of the key recurring concepts in Empedocles' philosophy: '...the elements only come together, and once mixed they divide'.

The intention of the Glass Bead Game is the realization of new work that relies on what Hesse describes as being a 'whole universe of possibilities and combinations' that becomes attainable for the individual player.

This new form is now realizable through new technology, which allows us to bring together music, the visual, and a wealth of resulting expression and ideas not previously possible (and much earlier than the 25th century setting of Hesse's novel) so that it's now possible to bring into existence things which were previously 'neither demonstrable nor probable'.

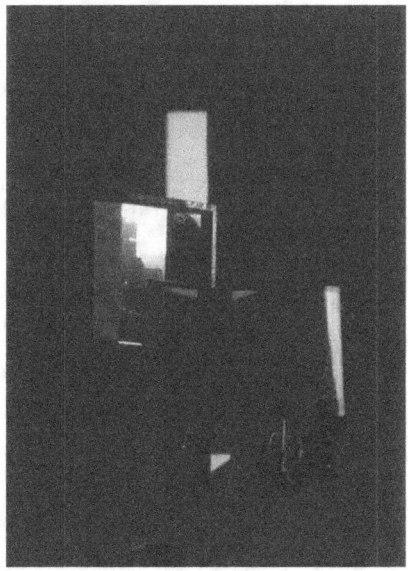

21. Havana morning

22. failed pictures

'- In the museums, for example, there are only pictures that have failed...

those which today we consider 'masterpieces' are those which departed most from the rules laid down by the masters of the period'.

Picasso believed that a finished picture was a dead picture, and there's an element of this aspect of his thinking here, regarding the 'masterpieces' in museums.

Also, what is a perfect picture exactly?

And what about the painting by Manet, *Musique aux Tuileries...Music in the Tuileries Gardens* (in the National Gallery, London) -

a work in which you can't tell what's there, right in the middle of the painting?

23. theorism

When does a practitioner for over 40 years (and still active) become a theorist?

When they write a book.

24. spatial/temporal orientation

Heard a newly composed orchestral piece on the radio this morning – it sounded like a work that had been composed four or even five decades ago.
When exactly was this piece going to end?

This goes to the heart of the problem of the 'atonal' approach to music, whereby the natural magnetic forces in pitches are overcome by an imposed abstract structure, which denies the existence of these forces, and so doesn't take advantage of their powers of attraction and repulsion, cycles of creation and destruction.

In a letter to his friend Josef Albers, Wassily Kandinsky drew a little sketch of a print he had been given by Albers: he was asking him what its title was. Kandinsky's sketch of this print (*Opera* was its title) is upside-down.

Spatial orientation and temporal orientation are intimately related: space and time are related in similar ways in both art and music.

In art, purely abstract work, whether something is the right way up or not, is a spatial problem to solve, just as in atonal music, knowing when a piece is going to end (effectively when to stop the music) is a similar problem, but in the dimension of time.

This is why tonality is related to the orientation of time in music, and figuration in art is related to the orientation of space.

(It's probably also the reason why drum improvisations in music can seem to last forever, and on the positive side, can put you into a trance).

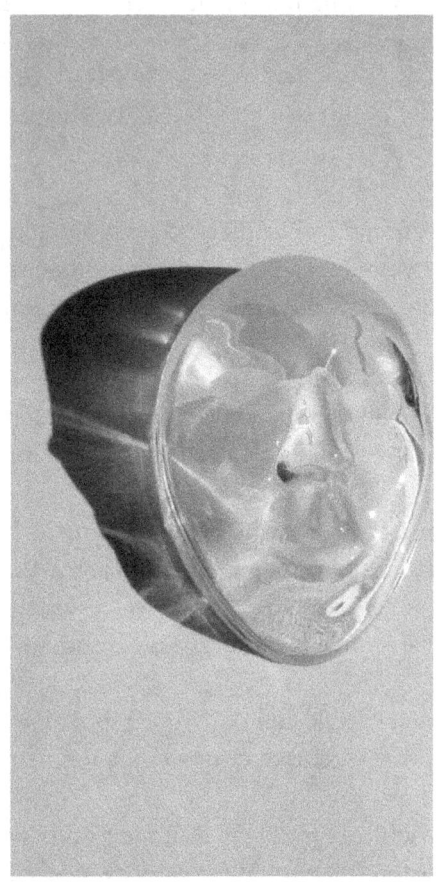

25. glass mask

26. *Breaking the Frame*

Invited by Marielle Nitoslawska to the London International Film Festival première of *Breaking the Frame*, her feature-length documentary film.

Breaking the Frame (2012) is an excellent example of the power of audiovisual cinema. Nitoslawska, in her portrait of Carolee Schneemann and her work, interweaves the visual with the equally varied and expressive music of James Tenney, who was a key person in Schneemann's life, both as partner and collaborator.

Breaking the Frame is also an unusual collaboration: in her introduction Nitoslawska told us how she worked closely with Carolee Schneemann on this film, and after the screening she explained the importance of her collaboration with her editor, Monique Dartonne.

In her film Nitoslawska also shows us less well-known examples of Schneemann's work, so we see how her early paintings relate to her famous films, like *Meat Joy* and *Fuses*, and how these works relate to her writings, and very evocative scrapbooks, the textures of which are captured so that one can almost touch and smell them.

We listen to Schneemann talking about her life and work, and Nitoslawska's own observations and responses are heard in the audiovisual weave of her film.

Early in the creative process, she was struck by the powerful atmosphere of Schneemann's New England farmhouse, full of mysterious dark spaces from which are unearthed things as varied as a chipmunk on a tray (freshly beheaded - a gift from the cat) or a box of poems typed on cards, which can be chance-ordered.

This is an artist's film, so Nitoslawaska, when she was faced with the extraordinary range of Schneemann's work, found ways to organise this proliferation: films, dance, performance, collages (in 2D and in 3D), paintings on snow and on canvas, poetry, installations.

Nitoslawska uses Schneemann's house as an evocative anchor for this variety, which includes the rhythms of the passing seasons, each bringing their own light to the surrounding wild landscape, and into the house.
Periodically a train passes by, rolling against the rhythms of the body and the changing weather.

The very process of organising the variety of material is part of Nitoslawska's film: at the end of *Breaking the Frame* we watch Schneemann as she organises the order of some of her photographic work, for a gallery show. She tries out various combinations for these big identically-sized works, which are still bubble-wrapped: so to us they remain as mysterious as the process of successfully organising a work of art itself.

27. Nimrud etc

Just returned from the British Museum, after a very amusing and informative talk about depictions on ancient Roman drinking cups and vases, given by a young specialist. He brought alive the possible thoughts a Roman might have had on viewing an image at the bottom of his very wide drinking cup, after having drunk the wine in it.
Nearby were displayed huge magnificent murals from Nimrud. This was the ancient city the 'Isis' fanatics have recently blown up. In retrospect, it was fortunate that the British had brought at least some of the massive statues and murals from Nimrud to London all those years ago.

Everyone depicted in these ancient murals looks sideways - a technique which has survived in cinematic convention to this day: 'Don't look at the camera!', the actors are told. As an audience we are god-like, we can be everywhere, but at the same time we must remain invisible.

And the subject of these murals? Battles. So what has changed?

28. *Working from Ignorance*

A walk around the notions of documentary and fact, in the company of a philosopher, a poet, an architect and a few painters

An expert is a man who has stopped thinking because 'he knows'.[1]

The documentary (film)
A factual film or television programme about an event, person, etc., presenting the facts with little or no fiction
Collins Dictionary of the English Language

Studying and making film at a Canadian film school in a city which is home to the Canadian Film Board, I have on several occasions been encouraged to think in terms of making a documentary film, or to consider the documentary film tradition in relation to my work. For some reason this has made me feel uncomfortable, but I haven't really been able to say *why* that clearly. Perhaps it's because I've spent most of my life as a composer, and the notions of 'documentary' and 'fact' don't really come up in composing music, in the same way as they do in the film medium. But now I've started making films perhaps it's time for me to confront this subject head-on, and to try and find out what makes me uncomfortable about the notion of making a documentary film. I should explain that the films I'm making are music/films where I'm responsible for composing both the film and the music - which work on an equal level in this form. However this shouldn't be an excuse for evading the question of my anxieties about working in the genre of the documentary.

Fact

The fact is a key part of the above dictionary definition of the film documentary: it would be hard to imagine a documentary without facts. It's likely that a documentary without facts would become something else altogether.

The idea of fact, as I understand it, is closely related to *what you know* to be the case. There's a strong element of certainty in this idea, and I've always been uncomfortable with the idea of certainty. It's too comfortable, too cosy a concept to get me interested in it. The fact is also related to the notion of what 'is', and therefore it's tied up with the idea of the 'real' and 'reality'. I am more interested in dealing with illusions.

In the front line trenches of World War 1, Wittgenstein was elaborating his *Tractatus Logico-Philosophicus*. Near the beginning of what he intended to be the end of philosophy, he wrote

1.2   The world divides into facts.[2]

One can understand why he thought this in the strange world of almost continuous shelling, machine-gun fire, and nights becoming like days because of the intensity of the bombardments. It's an environment where there must have been little room for illusions.[3]

'Write What You Know'

In the quieter and superficially calmer world of present-day Montreal, I thought I'd look at the notion of fact from the angle of 'what you know'. As documentary films rely heavily on scripts, this led me to look at writing, to investigate what the experts on writing believe is important. Then this led me to looking at current books which offer advice to those who wish to learn to write. Could this provide me with a 'way in' to understanding my problem with the documentary form? I remembered the 'write *what you know*' advice from a course for beginner-playwrights I'd read about some time ago. More recently I found a similar statement in a book about what you should know about writing – there's an acknowledgement that the 'write what you know' advice is a well-worn cliché, but the author assures us that it's still valid, even if you have a fertile and vivid imagination, as your writing will be the best, about what you know the best.

Looking at the various 'how to write' books in a bookstore, I couldn't help noticing that they were all by writers (and a poet - for a book on how to write poetry) who don't seem to be known as writers, other than writing a published book on how to write. Is it for this reason that they hardly quote from their *own* writing?

How Are Verses Made?

I decided to look up a book on how to write by someone who became known for his writing, though he's almost forgotten today. I picked up a copy of Mayakovsky's *How Are Verses Made? (Kak delat' stikhi, 1926)*. In it he actually refers to the ancestors of the type of books I found in the bookstore. He mentions people who wish to make money from those who want to learn to write:

Here, for instance, is an advert from the Kharkov Proletarian (No. 256)

'How do you become a writer?

Send 50 kopecks in stamps for details. Slavyansk, on the Donets railway, Box number 11.'

Handy, isn't it?! [4]

Throughout *How Are Verses Made?* Mayakovsky refers to his own poetry and the circumstances which caused him to write various poems. He was probably the best known and most visible poet of the Russian Revolution, so he frequently refers to the inspiration he found in contemporary political struggles - he even mentions the importance of the documentary fact. As an example, he gives us the documentary reports which are written by the peasants' and workers' journalists, which are of great interest to him, and which he values above what he describes as 'so-called poetical works'.[5]

However, no matter how hard you look in *How Are Verses Made?* you won't find Mayakovsky confusing the idea of a fact with what makes a poem. He pinpoints for him the danger in writing what you know, which was highlighted by a period of 'writer's block', when for around three months he would return again and again to his subject, without being able to think of writing anything sensible. Then he realised that his problem of a lack of inspiration was due to there being too close a correspondence between his situation and what he wished to write about. As examples from his life at the time, he mentions 'the same hotel rooms, the same water-pipes, the same enforced solitude'.[6]

In other words, being too close to just the plain facts.

From this frustrating experience, he finds 'what is almost a rule'. In order to write poetry, you have to have 'a change of place or of time'. Mayakovsky explains that the greater the importance of what you are writing about, the more distance from it you must have. He states that 'feeble people mark time' and wait for an event to take place and to pass them by, so that they are in a position to describe it, but 'the strong run forward just far enough to seize the event and draw it towards them.'[7]

This is why the energy of imagination that Mayakovsky had as a political poet could also be useful to him as a love poet:

In order to write about the tenderness of love, take bus No. 7 from the Lubyansky Square to Nogin Square. The appalling jolting will serve to throw into relief for you, better than anything else, the charm of a life transformed. A shake-up is essential, for the purposes of comparison.[8]

He describes the origin of the title of one of his best known longer poems. He was returning to Moscow from Saratov in around 1913, to prove his devotion to 'a certain female companion', and he tells her that he is 'not a man, but a cloud in trousers.' As soon as he says this, he realises that he could use this striking image in a poem, which he did, two years later, when he needed a title for one of his long poems: *A Cloud in Trousers*.[9]

In what way is 'a cloud in trousers' a fact? Was Mayakovsky writing about something he knew? Or could it have been because he had an energy of imagination? It was 'vivid and fertile', the qualities mentioned and mildly disparaged by the author of the self-confirmed clichéd advice offered to writers.

The automatic solution

Fortunately most of the other books that I found on how to write avoided the 'write about what you know' cliché by resorting to the technique of tapping into your subconscious via automatic writing. The Surrealist origin of this method is never mentioned, perhaps because Surrealism might be associated with the weird by some readers, and therefore commercially not viable. It seems to me that this problem has to do with what subject the beginner artist should choose to write about/paint/sculpt/film. It is a question of content. In a way, I feel that automatic writing (or its visual equivalent) is slightly dishonest advice, as it bypasses the question of the problem of content, which at least the 'write what you know' cliché appears to solve instantly.

The problem of content

An artist who was overtly concerned with the problem of content, the problem of *what* to paint, what subject matter should be addressed, was Barnett Newman. Thomas B. Hess, in his book on the artist, mentions that when Newman
named an art school, he called it 'The Subjects of the Artist'; what else is there for a serious student to learn? [10]

Hess explains earlier that
Newman spent his first twenty-two years as an artist in search for his subject matter (...) He always insisted on its crucial importance (...) it was the single element that distinguished the artist from the decorator or craftsman (...) it implicated the deepest content of art, what it **is**.[11]

In this instance, one could say that the painting has become its own subject matter. Newman, in his text *The Plasmic Image*, explains what he is attempting to achieve in painting. He distances himself from Surrealist automatism, for him *Surrealism is interested in a dream world that will penetrate the human psyche,* while he himself is not concerned *with his own feelings or with the mystery of his own personality but with the penetration into the world mystery.* By attempting *to go beyond the visible and the known world, he is working with forms that are unknown even to him.* In this way he is *engaged in a true act of discovery in the creation of new forms and symbols that will have the living quality of creation.*[12]

In 1965 Picasso said that for his part, he was never troubled by the problem of content: *the subject, that never scared me.*[13] He takes what we think we know, for example roosters:
like everything else in life we must discover them. (...) Everything must be discovered - this box - a piece of paper. Picasso then states that you should always *leave the door open,* and above all you should never turn back through it: you should never dismay, or compromise. And he adds that *roosters have always been seen but seldom so well as in American weather vanes.*[14]

So Picasso shares with Barnett Newman the desire to discover, to go beyond the *known world*, to something which lies *beyond* what they know, to make something which has *the living quality of creation*. With Newman it's finding new subjects, with Picasso it's often to do with rediscovering old subjects, like roosters.

Discovery is the process of finding uncertainties in what appears to be the most certain. It can only begin with a confession of ignorance, a position of lack of knowledge, or of uncertainty, or even of doubt. This is why testing is an essential part of the process of discovery, as is error and chance. It's also question of being aware of illusions.

Each day is really a voyage into the unknown: the idea that you know something is a fiction. By the time you have written what you know, what you know is probably obsolete - things have moved on already.

Chagall, in his autobiography puts it very succinctly:
...we really are up in the air and suffer from one disease alone: the thirst for stability.[15]

Accelerated change

One can understand the idea of a thirst for stability amongst those artists and thinkers who were born in the 19th century, who survived two world wars and lived into the second half of the 20th century. They all had first-hand experience of the accelerated changes brought about by these wars and the accompanying scientific developments. In 1949, in conversation with Oets Bouwsma, another philosopher of the same age as him, Wittgenstein remarked that his parents in Vienna *would scarcely recognise this as the same world.*

Bouwsma refers to the obvious development of machines in the 20th century, but he points out that Wittgenstein was rather thinking about how people had changed, how they had become more complex. Before, lives were simpler and more stable: people lived in one house, they had access to certain tools, they owned a domesticated animal, and they would know well a small group of local people. This kind of life was both simple and stable, and so people would become attached to their roots, within this narrow environment. Now, people are more transient, and consequently communities change, and so we are no longer sentimentally attached to the area in which we live.[16]

At about the same time (1951) Frank Lloyd Wright, aged 84, was concerned with similar questions. At Taliesin he asked his students about the speed of the development of machines.

He gives an example of the way that the car has left behind human values, and a moral sense that was related to the way of life that existed before the invention of the internal combustion engine. Wright mentions a man who now owns something which is a deadly menace and which he hasn't been educated to control properly: his car. He explains that before using this (what then was) new technology to get around, this man would have trudged along, shouldering a stick with a bundle attached to it - now he whirls along in a cloud of dust. Wright affirms that this man is *more deadly now and no more competent than he was in the days of the Egyptians*, and he adds: *as it applies to him, it applies to society, it applies to the world.*[17]

Both Lloyd Wright's and Wittgenstein's thinking on accelerated change and its consequences were possible because they had lived through this period of accelerated change: these transformations had impinged on their consciousness and they had in both cases played an active role in creating them. Lloyd Wright had a passion for foreign fast cars and he apparently wasn't as safe a driver as one might have expected - he would, even in later years, drive cars like the Mercedes-Benz and the Jaguar, at frightening speeds.[18]

But he was also responsible for a complete change in thinking about architecture, and its practice, both domestic and public. Wittgenstein had a comparably huge influence on philosophy. Like Lloyd Wright, he continues to be an influence today, but in Wittgenstein's case, I believe that we are still not fully aware of the extent of his achievements. It's also easy to forget that at various times in his life he was involved as a practitioner in a wide variety of tasks: for example he compiled a dictionary for elementary schools, he designed and supervised the building of a large house in Vienna. At Manchester University, aged 21 (seven years after the first Wright brothers' flight) he had already developed and patented an aircraft engine, based on a jet-propulsion principle. As Ray Monk describes in his biography of the philosopher, this engine turned out not to be practical for aeroplane propulsion, but during the Second World War it was successfully used in certain types of helicopter.[19]

Wittgenstein described Jim Bamber, who assisted him with his experiments at Manchester University, as being one of the few people with whom he had got on well at that time. Bamber remembered how Wittgenstein would *swear volubly in German*, wave his arms about and stamp around, when things were not going right, which apparently happened quite often.[20]

He was obviously not working with only what he knew.

When Wittgenstein was thinking about the nature of colour, (using the numbered propositions he continued to use after his *Tractatus*) he wrote on the 28th March 1950:

44. (…) In any serious question uncertainty extends to the very roots of the problem.

*45. One must always be prepared to learn something **totally** new.*[21]

Ray Monk mentions that when Wittgenstein was invited to Cornell University in 1949, he would often take long walks in the nearby countryside and was fascinated by the local flora, unfamiliar to him. On one occasion, he got caught in bad weather and he accepted a lift from a colleague of the professor who had invited him to Cornell. He had found some seed pods which the driver identified as milkweed seeds, and to satisfy Wittgenstein's curiosity, he had stopped to pick some milkweed flowers. Then Wittgenstein *looked in awe from flowers to seed pods and from seed pods to flowers. Suddenly he crumpled them up, threw them down on the floor of the car, and trampled them. 'Impossible!' he said.*[22]

This ability to be open to new experience, to directly face things which are beyond one's knowledge was also a characteristic of Frank Lloyd Wright, another who was profoundly affected and influenced by the complex structures of plants, trees, and other organic forms, in his case, in his architecture.

The architect Peter Blake describes the official doubts about the mushroom-like slender tapered columns Wright had designed in 1936 as the basic structural unit for the Johnson Wax building in Racine, Wisconsin. Nobody had come across a structure like this before, so that nobody (except Wright) believed that the structure would stand up. When a test column was erected and tested with sandbags to the point of destruction, the engineers were astonished and baffled that the slender column was capable of bearing many times the loads for which it had been designed.[23]

However there is another side to this. An architect who specialises in the maintenance of Lloyd Wright buildings (literally hundreds of the buildings he designed still exist) told me in 1999 that a spire at the Florida Southern College (part of the campus designed by Wright) collapsed at least five times when it was being built.[24] Another architect told me last year that he was disappointed to see iron scaffolding poles propping up a wing of Fallingwater, on a recent visit to Wright's daringly cantilevered building.[25] Donald Hoffman, in his account of the construction of Fallingwater describes the numerous tests needed to resolve the problems the structural engineers had with the cantilevers exceeding allowable stress, and Wright's corresponding modifications of his original plans.[26]

What we see here relates to the question of the degree of risk involved: going far enough beyond the known, yet making sure that the limits of safety are not exceeded. Though Lloyd Wright's self-confidence was legendary, he must have known that going beyond what he already knew would incur the risk of error and just being wrong.

In looking at these questions, one seems again and again to be dealing with what would work 'in reality'. This is a result of a century when the speed of technological development, accelerated by war, brought about fundamental changes, highlighting our ignorance about our understanding of anything, from the moral implications of the internal combustion engine, the mechanism of various types of jet propulsion, the workable limits of the cantilever, to the mechanics of the transformation of the structure of a flower into the structure of a seed pod. This also relates back to the idea of the existence of the fact, of the value of what one knows or considers to be a fact, in other words what one believes reality to be. And this again relates to the question of content, which is why I'm going to look at what two very different 20th century painters said about the concept of reality.

Reality

This is such a slippery word, I thought I'd see what a tremendously concrete painter like Picasso said about it:

There are so many realities that in trying to encompass them all one ends in darkness.

It's for this reason that Picasso explains that when you paint a portrait, you have to stop at some point, *in a sort of caricature.* If you don't do this, then *there would be nothing left at the end.*[27]

It's interesting that Picasso's view of reality is not single and static, but that it forms a dynamic plurality. This dynamism comes through when he referred to it again, this time in a conversation with Françoise Gilot:

What interests me is to make what might be called links, connections, over the widest possible distance - the most unexpected links between objects I wish to consider. One must rip and tear reality.[28]

Though it's now briefly in the singular, Picasso rips up reality into multiple forms.

His reference to *the widest possible distance* echoes what Mayakovsky was saying earlier. And *a cloud in trousers* is for me an effective link *over the widest possible distance.*

Josef Albers, a very different painter, who appears to be much calmer than Picasso, went even further than Picasso, when the concept of the reality in his painting was put to him:

What is reality? This word I never get into my vocabulary.[29]

Red and Blue

It's interesting to compare both painters' comments about the slippery reality of colour.

Albers points out that if he says the word 'red' to an audience of fifty people, then it's highly likely that each person in that audience will internally see a very different red – at least fifty shades of red will be imagined. He goes on to demonstrate that this phenomenon even applies to well known brand colours, which have to be the same whenever they appear. As an example, Albers gives the shade of red which is used in Coca-Cola signs. Even if this very specific colour is mentioned to the audience, Albers tells us that each person in it will nevertheless still think of a different shade of this particular red. And he goes further: even if he shows the audience hundreds of shades of red, and he asks them to identify which one is the Coca-Cola red, then they will still choose very different shades, and even then, nobody will be certain that they will have chosen the exact Coca Cola shade of red.[30]

Picasso is equally clear about the instability of our perception of colour. In his case he takes blue as an example:

'Blue' - what does 'blue' mean? There are thousands of sensations that we call 'blue'.

He mentions the blue on a packet of *Gauloise* cigarettes, or *the Gauloise blue of eyes*, or in another very different case in a restaurant in Paris, you can ask that your steak be 'blue', when in fact you mean that you want it to be red.[31]

Frank Lloyd Wright also had an intriguing comment about the nature of colour itself:

The element of color – it is another world. That probably is the most mysterious world of all – even more mysterious than form.[32]

The cinema of reality

When Bouwsma mentioned to Wittgenstein the famous statement by Descartes: *I think, therefore I am*, Wittgenstein thought of an analogy which I find intriguing, because it introduces the idea of time into what I think is a consideration of the notion of reality:

I always think of it as like the cinema. You see before you the picture on the screen, but behind you is the operator, and he has a roll here on this side from which he is winding and another on that side into which he is winding. The present is the picture which is before the light, but the future is still on this roll to pass, and the past is on that roll. It's gone through already. Now imagine that there is only the present. There is no future roll, and no past roll. And now further imagine what language there could be in such a situation. One could just gape. This!* [33] I experienced something like this recently when an acquaintance of mine, the publisher and musician Morris Kahn, was showing me the view of the internal courtyard from his flat, with its hanging baskets of flowers. He said that film companies sometimes used it as a location for Spanish-style exteriors. He paused, held out the palms of his hands towards this view, and shrugged simultaneously. For me this was more eloquent than any words could have been in this situation.

Returning just for a moment to Wittgenstein's film analogy, I found a paradoxical statement along similar lines by Picasso:

Art has no past, or future. Art which is not in the present will never exist.[34]

The Canon

The people I have mentioned again and again are frequently called *the canon*.

Perhaps I should be bothered by this, but actually I'm not. What *does* concern me is the way in which whole areas of knowledge, of experience, are shut out and ignored because *the canon* is treated like a monument which is passed every day without a single glance, because of its overwhelmingly static characteristics. The grey inertia of the monument is caused by the static, closed-off interpretation of these artists' achievements, which can result in grey thought, or worse, a grey consciousness.

This was something which concerned Picasso about his own work. Pierre Daix, one of his biographers, tells us that Picasso would understandably be very angry when visitors to his studio would praise him, without bothering to look at his work: *What have I done to deserve this treatment?* he would ask - *Why do they treat me like an historic monument?* [35]

He could also see another side to the problem of the canon's morbid immobility:

Art is not the application of a canon of beauty but what the instinct and the brain can conceive beyond any canon.[36]

Grey consciousness

This is why the notion of a canon is not one that I find helpful or useful. The idea of an accepted criterion, which is part of the concept of the canon, I associate with the graveyard aspect of the archive, with its dusty, over-classified, unvisited vaults, a repository of grey consciousness.

Bouwsma expresses something along similar lines, when he describes how, in retrospect, Wittgenstein *robbed me of a lazy comfort in my own mediocrity.*[37]

This was the type of mental laziness I had with regard to Picasso. I remember in the Sixties how there had been a falling-off in his reputation, reflected in comments in the newspapers which suggested that the artist's work of the time was either the product of a senile and impotent charlatan, or of someone who was something of a 'has-been.' Daix gives many examples of this *underestimation, even rejection* by critics of Picasso's output of this time.[38]

Then, later, a visit I made to the Picasso Museum in Paris created a brief enthusiasm, but one which faded - his work seemed too cerebral. Perhaps it was the formal nature of the typical Parisian *hôtel,* perhaps there was too much of a feeling of the grey monument in that building. Then there was the revelation of the exhibition of Picasso's sculptures at the Tate Gallery in 1994. But its formality somehow killed off the energy and humour of his work - perhaps these sculptures would work best in a less neat environment, more akin to Picasso's chaotic studios. I think that it was for this reason that a visit to the Château Grimaldi in Antibes last year finally destroyed the concept of the Picasso canon for me.

The Château Grimaldi

The huge rambling rooms of this medieval castle have great thick walls harboring windows opening to the bright Mediterranean Sea. It has an interior plan which is far from obvious, an ideal setting for Picasso's work from this time, the years immediately following the end of World War II. The Château Grimaldi's curator, Dor de la Souchère, as a result of a chance meeting with Picasso on the beach, offered the artist the use of part of this Château - it was an inspired decision.

Somehow Picasso's happiness and optimism from that time radiated from the work on show, it was almost as if he were there, his energy was present. Subsequently I found out why I'd felt this. Daix believes that *in this new phase of his life, when more than ever he was staking his future in art, Picasso was also placing a bet on the unforeseeable, the unknown.*[39]

New media, new forms

It was also at this time, when Picasso, aged 65, decided to work in a medium completely new to him: ceramics, and there he found an astonishing range of creative possibilities. He was particularly delighted by the *constantly renewed surprises of transmutation of oxides, ceramic slips, and colours experienced by the enamels as they went through the baking process.* His newly acquired technical skills in this medium enabled him to shake up tradition, *even if the local pottery workers didn't always appreciate Picasso's jolting effect on their methods.*[40]

Ten years later, in his mid-seventies, he began his first linocuts, starting with the *Buste de femme d'après Cranach le Jeune*. He used six states for this work, each one etched with different details and reserved for a different colour, in itself a virtuoso technical achievement. He would then assess the unpredictable effects of the colour combinations which arose from this complex process.[41]

In his late eighties he went on to experiment with technical transpositions between painting, engraving, ceramics and sculpting. Excited by his innovations in engraving, he discovered that he could also apply these new techniques to his painting.[42]

Already, in 1956, Picasso had spoken of his research-like approach, echoing for me Wittgenstein's thinking technique - numbering and dating each proposition:

I never do a painting as a work of art. All of them are researches. I search incessantly and there is a logical sequence in all this research. That is why I number them. It's an experiment in time. I number them and date them. Maybe one day someone will be grateful, he added laughingly.[43]

The neatly planned city

This capacity Picasso had for continually developing, catching himself out, and starting over, even in advanced years, is the opposite of a neatly planned enterprise, followed by a successful conclusion.

In 1946 when Jaime Sabartés pointed out to Picasso that he had made several spelling errors in something the artist had written, we see in the painter's response ideas which I feel relate strongly to all of Picasso's output, in whatever medium he chose to work:

"So what? From errors one gets to know the personality! If I were to start correcting the mistakes you mention in accordance with rules which have nothing to do with me, whatever is personal in my writings would be lost in a grammar which I have not assimilated. I would prefer to invent a grammar of my own than to bind myself to rules which do not belong to me." [44]

It's the opposite of the notion of the accepted criterion, which characterises the idea of the canon, of grey thinking. Frank Lloyd Wright put it very succinctly to Edgar Tafel: *what we did yesterday we won't do today. And what we don't do tomorrow will not be what we'll be doing the day after.* [45] This ability to continuously re-evaluate oneself brings to mind another who also had this capacity to continually re-think, in abundance.

When Wittgenstein was questioned about belief and illusion

He was quiet for several minutes. Then he said: It's like this:

In the city, streets are nicely laid out. And you drive on the right and you have traffic lights, etc. There are rules. When you leave the city, there are still roads, but no traffic lights. And when you get far off there are no roads, no lights, no rules, nothing to guide you. It's all woods. And when you return to the city you may feel that the rules are wrong, that there should be no rules, etc[46]

I am finding Wittgenstein's city analogy particularly evocative and useful, as I'm currently making a music/film which relates to Montreal in winter. I have found that sometimes the winter transforms the neat streets into something not city-like at all: the pavements disappear, the cars disappear, there is hardly anyone around. Most life retreats into comforting hibernation, away from the brutality of the weather outside. The wilderness which normally lies safely far away, outside the city, makes a trip to visit its heart. During its wild and unpredictable residence the rules of the neat and ordered summer city no longer apply. It makes such an impact that even in the summer city you can detect the debris of its effect.

These experiences are relatively new to me, as is the medium in which I'm working: music and film. Consequently, in making this music/film (which isn't a documentary) I know I'll be working from ignorance, and hopefully coming up against an exciting wilderness of errors, illusions, uncertainties and doubts.

1 *Frank Lloyd Wright on Architecture, Nature, and the Human Spirit: A Collection of Quotations*, ed. Bruce Brooks Pfeiffer, Pomegranate Europe, 2011, p. 49
2 Wittgenstein, Ludwig, *Tractatus logico-Philosophicus*, trs Pears, D.F. & McGuinness, B.F., Routledge & Kegan Paul, London and Henley, 1974, pp. 4-5
3 Monk, Ray, *Ludwig Wittgenstein, The Duty of Genius*, Vintage, London, 1991, p.137ff
4 Mayakovsky, Vladimir, *How Are Verses Made?*, trs Hyde, G.M., Jonathan Cape, London, 1970, p.26
5 Ibid. p.34
6 Ibid. p.32
7 Ibid. p.33

8 Ibid. p.35
9 Ibid. pp.24-25
10 Hess, Thomas B., *Barnett Newman*, in Tate Gallery catalogue, London, 1972, p.8
11 Ibid.
12 Ibid., pp.22-23
13 Ashton, Dore, *Picasso on Art: A Selection of Views*, Thames & Hudson, London, 1972, p.36
14 Ibid., pp.34-35
15 Chagall, Marc, *My Life*, Oxford University Press, Oxford, New York, 1989, p.171
16 Bouwsma, O.K., *Wittgenstein, Conversations 1949-1951*, ed.by Craft, J.L. and Hustwit, Ronald E., Hackett Publishing Company, Indianapolis, 1986, p.39
17 Frank Lloyd Wright, in discussion with his Fellowship students on the theme of machines and morality, audiocassette recording, 1951. *Machinery and Mankind* (11022), J. Norton Publishers, (1976) c1952.
18 Secrest, Meryle, *Frank Lloyd Wright, A Biography*, Chatto & Windus,London, 1992, p.488
19 Monk, *Wittgenstein*, p.33
20 Ibid., p.34
21 Wittgenstein, Ludwig, *Remarks on Colour*, ed.by Anscombe, G.E.M., trs McAlister, Linda L., & Schattle, Margarete. Basil Blackwell, Oxford, 1977, p.23e
22 Monk: *Wittgenstein*, pp.552-553.
    Wittgenstein knew Goethe's *Metamorphosis of Plants*, in which Goethe shows how the various organs of plants are related, and how they transform into each other. (Monk, *Wittgenstein*, pp 303, 304) Also, in his *Introduction to Comparative Anatomy*, Goethe writes that *the organic parts of a plant ... are all identical organs which a succession of vegetative operations modifies and transforms beyond recognition. (Goethe: Wisdom and Experience*, Routledge and Kegan Paul, trans. Hermann J. Weigand, London,1949)
23 Blake, Peter, *Frank Lloyd Wright, Architecture and Space*, Penguin Books Ltd., Harmondsworth, 1963, p.100
24 The British architect John McAslan.
25 Chris Tweed, at Queen's University, Belfast

26 Hoffman, Donald, *Frank Lloyd Wright's Fallingwater, The House and its History*, Dover Publications, Inc., New York, 1978, p.41ff
27 Ashton, *Picasso on Art*, p.27
28 Daix, Pierre, *Picasso: Life and Art*, Thames & Hudson, London, 1994, pp.270-271
29 Albers, Josef, Exploring the Dialectic of the Eye. Audiocassette, North Hollywood, CA, Centre for Cassette Studies 27605, ca 1974
30 Albers, Josef, *Interaction of Color*, Yale University Press, New Haven and London, 1975, p.3
31 Ashton, *Picasso on Art*, p.131
32. *Frank Lloyd Wright on Architecture, Nature, and the Human Spirit*, ed. Bruce Brooks Pfeiffer, The Frank Lloyd Wright Foundation, 2011, p.62.
33 Bouwsma, O.K., *Wittgenstein, Conversations*, p.13
34 Daix, Pierre, *Picasso: Life and Art*, p.377
35 Ibid., p.285
36 Ashton, *Picasso on Art*, p.73
37 Bouwsma, O.K., *Wittgenstein, Conversations*, p.xvi
38 Daix, Pierre, *Picasso: Life and Art*, p.349 and p.355ff
39 Ibid., p.292
40 Ibid., pp.298-299
41 Ibid., p.341
42 Ibid., p.361
43 Ashton, *Picasso on Art*, p.72
44 Ibid., pp.45-46
45 Secrest, Meryle, *Frank Lloyd Wright*, p.443
46 Bouwsma, O.K., *Wittgenstein, Conversations*, p.35

29. a unique gallery

Last Saturday I was in a delightful gallery/screening/talks/discussion/music café called the Hundred Years Gallery, at 13 Pearson Street in Hoxton, East London.

The artist Montse Gallego set up the gallery, and named it after the novel by Gabriel García Márquez, *One Hundred Years of Solitude*.

She directs it, along with musician Graham MacKeachan, who organizes the very active international new music programme there.

Its atmosphere is convivial - there's intriguing art on the walls: halved violins and various invented instruments, then more recently, computer animated art on screens, which downstairs in the basement develops into light sculptures, an installation with light pulsing down wires in all directions, and images on a screen which can be controlled by a console and a keyboard. Upstairs in the café you can see someone taking a book from a display and sitting with it in one of the sofas there to read it, in this case *The Quadrivium*. The books that are lying around relate to the art on display at the time, an excellent and stimulating idea. In fact you probably won't leave this unique gallery without having had an interesting discussion, a read, or an encounter with a film, or improvised music, or poets performing their work, or if you stay long enough, all of these.

The River That Walks was shown there earlier this year, and was shown again last Saturday, preceded by *Oserake*, courtesy of Montse and Graham. It was shown on the biggest screen it's ever been projected on, along with a varied selection of films, which featured choreography, various audiovisual techniques, and flute music, Japanese and European. Chris H. Lynn's *People's Park Reverie*, with its rhythms of summer in a Shanghai public park, and its musical colours, also worked really well on the huge screen – you felt you were right there looking at the green sunlight through the swaying giant lotus leaves on the lake.

The River That Walks was also shown in January, at Baxter's Gallery in Cowcross Street, London, as part of the annual symposium of the Landscape and Arts Network. The presentations were monitored by a splendid lady, who struck a lithophone if anyone exceeded their 15-minute slot: it's more civilised than striking the speaker with the beater.

30. the sales pitch

With this technology you are only limited by your imagination!

But your imagination is limited, just like it's only feasible to be involved with a relatively small part of the globe on a daily basis.

In Montreal, I noticed that the news and weather were circumscribed by an area going as far as Burlington, but no further.

And the international news was just as limited, but in another way.

As humans we can't work easily with an area much beyond certain geographical limits, on an everyday basis.

In London you have London news, like a bee has news of a specific area it has been allotted to gather pollen and nectar to make honey.

In the human sphere of activity, the news is also specific to you as an individual - the international news, extremely and selectively distilled by the journalists, works on the same principle, which determines our limited capacity as individuals to absorb and transmit vast quantities of relevant information.

31. perceptions

Artists like Hokusai, da Vinci,
writers like Joyce and Dostoyevsky,
composers like J.S. Bach, Mozart, Beethoven,
don't only paint, write or compose to commission,
or just paint, write, and compose –
they are using the mastery of their medium to
re-create their perceptions of the world.

32. *The Drunken Boat*

    I remember a very boring seminar, for the French Literature part of my degree.

Everyone seemed to be half asleep - we were supposed to be analysing *Le bateau ivre*, the famous poem by Arthur Rimbaud.

Suddenly the lecturer turns to the sleepiest student, asking me:

'Mr Robertson, what is happening at this point in the poem?

I look at the relevant line.

'At this point' I replied, 'the poet appears to want to drown'.

33. emotions

    Emotions are no more primary than colours.

34. Dad's Army

This excellent comedy series has been remade into a film.

Imagine Eisenstein endlessly remaking *The Battleship Potemkin*, with multiple variations of the 'Odessa Steps' section.

This is the equivalent of today's bankruptcy of the imagination.

Innovation, true innovation has become conceptually invisible now, a hamburgerisation of the mind.

35. mapping the brain

There are those who really believe that by mapping the brain and locating its functions, they can understand how it works.

They might as well learn as much about people, simply by naming places on a map, and so differentiating one location from another - they won't get much closer to understanding the people who live in those places: these people's histories, their complex lives and interactions.

And anyway they forget that they're using their own brains to map the brains of others, which is another powerful limitation: they're using a map to map the map.

36. prize

Some time ago I won an international book prize for a book about Eisenstein.

Bravo!

As a result this book is in over a thousand libraries worldwide.

Bravo! Bravo!

And it's read by student filmmakers, and filmmakers worldwide.

Bravo! Bravo! Bravo!

And it's hated by Eisenstein specialists worldwide.

Bravo! Bravo!

Fortunately there aren't many of them.

Bravo! Bravo! Bravo! Bravo!

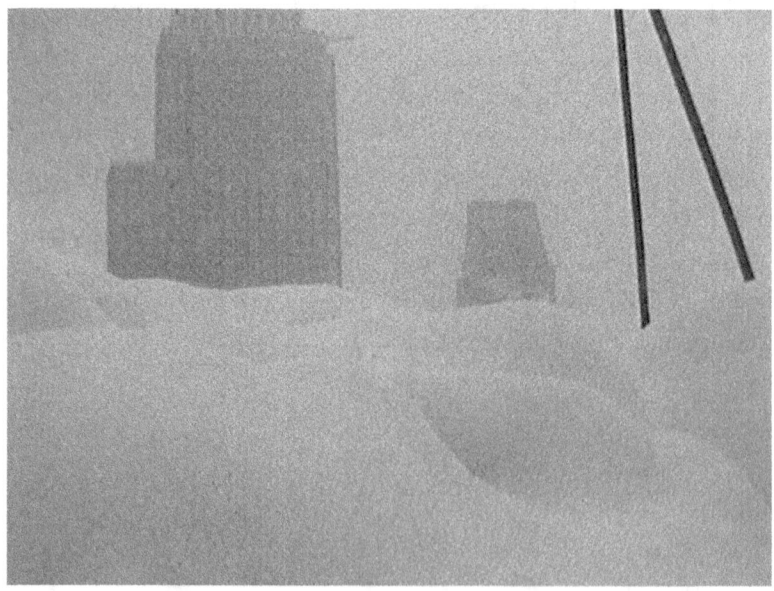

37. Montreal snow

38. not illustrations

I have really never made illustrations for anything. There are pieces of mine that have been put with texts with which they more or less fit.

39. different countries

Physically we live in different countries, and we largely have no idea about what is really happening in them, even in this time of instant communication.

But in addition we live in different countries of the mind.

This means that we can also have no idea of what is happening in the country in which we live, or even in the same city.

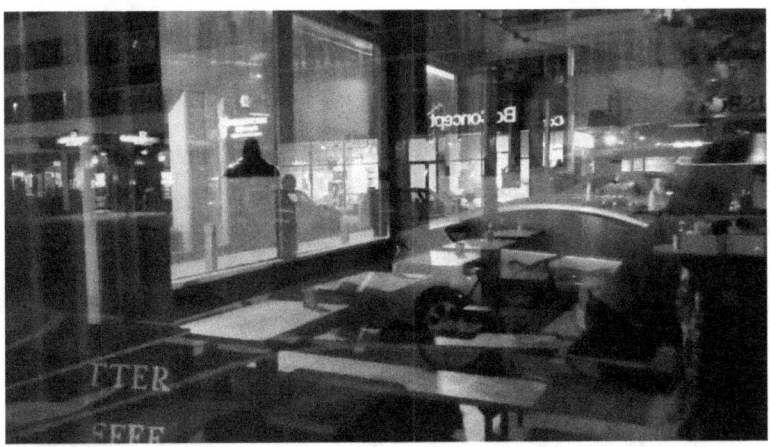

40. after hours

41. deciphering ancient manuscripts

I like going to music master-classes.

The classical musicians in these events usually wear their everyday clothes, not the livery of servants, as in formal concerts – I like that informality.

Today, the well-known early music conductor, viol player and composer Jordi Savall will be helping some student viol players in music mostly from the Baroque era and a little later: music by Georg Philipp Telemann, Marin Marais, C.P.E. Bach, Carl Friedrich Abel, and Antoine Forqueray.

Early in the class Jordi Savall mentions that in Beethoven's time, the performance indication *Alla gamba* ('As in the viola da gamba') was used to describe what today is called *Sul ponticello* ('play near the bridge of the instrument'). This point is a memorable way to underline the importance of the wonderfully resonant sound of the viola da gamba, whereby this characteristically rich sound of the instrument is achieved by playing closer to the bridge, and away from the finger-board, which produces a rather drier and less colourful sound.

The way in which the bow is used, and how it should be drawn against the string comes up next: Savall points out the key importance of relaxation, in order to be able to control the instrument. He urges the performer to be more confident, to look away from the instrument, not always to be wrapped tensely around it: 'don't add tension to tension' he says. The movement of the hand holding the bow should accompany the movement of the arm, and the wrist must be flexible. Any tension must be introduced in a controllable way, through the context of the whole body of the performer being in a relaxed state in the first place. Savall says that the bow is like a brush for a painter: it's gestural, but controlled.

I remembered in a concert watching the jazz violinist Stéphane Grappelli perform: he was completely relaxed, confident, and in complete control of the instrument. He wasn't just holding the violin, it was a natural and organic extension of his body.

'Play like you know yourself' Savall emphasises. Playing an instrument is a form of self-expression, and so it's an intrinsic part of a process of self-knowledge. 'If you are tense, you can't control your energy – if you are tense the energy is dissipated' he says.

Breathing is another key aspect of performance. Savall advises the performer to take a breath before playing: the way you breathe when playing music is an intrinsic part of playing an instrument. Savall explains that in its time, the viola da gamba was described as being the most expressive musical instrument, second only to the voice. He encourages the student to sing the phrases in the music, and he stresses that a musician must imagine what she or he wants to do, before doing it. He urges the musician to 'play with your whole body' – of course this also involves being able to express with your voice what you will play.

Savall wants the students to concentrate on expression in their playing – he wants them to extend their expressivity. He explains that this music is like talking to someone. The performers should express something *through* their playing, and not just play the notes. More variety is needed in the dynamic range between loud and soft, more expression, more emotion.

The students play a sarabande, but the yearning sensuality of this dance is absent. Savall notes that this style of performance is 'dusty' – it's rigid, rather than relaxed and gracefully enthusiastic. He asks for more definition in the rhythms, so that the sarabande doesn't become a formless 'sonic sauce'. To demonstrate this, he sings the sarabande's main melodic line, with a clearly expressed rhythmic articulation. Savall summarises what is happening here: 'the emotion makes the memory, the memory makes the spirit'.

He reminds the students that the pieces that they have played are dances, so that the performers should move accordingly. This sounds obvious to rock and pop musicians, but as much Baroque music is actually dance music, the performers at the time would not just have played this music, but on other occasions would have danced to music on which these dances were based. Does this mean that today's early music performers of Baroque music need to learn how to dance the allemandes, courantes, gigues, and other such dances from this period?

This question brought me back to memories of a Sunday afternoon dance in the countryside near Cap-Haïtien, in Haïti. I'd come across it when I was doing research for *The Kingdom* in the summer of 1981. Here, the relationship between the drummer and the dancers is both direct and reciprocal – the villagers know the dances, and the drummer knows exactly when to move from one dance to another, and to move not only in terms of the characteristic rhythm of each particular dance, but also to move himself along with his drum, dancing along with it, even though it was too big an instrument to be easily portable (like the viola da gamba). The dancing, the drumming and the singing are as one: a single expressive entity, uniting body, breath, sound and song.

42. the kye-nee-ma

I was invited by Dr Emma Widdis, Reader in Russian Studies at Trinity College, Cambridge, to give a talk on Eisenstein's ideas on the audiovisual.

Offered an overnight stay at a flat near the College, I had breakfast at Trinity, and got a sense of what Eisenstein experienced when he had lunch at High Table: he and Ivor Montagu had been invited by the Soviet physicist Peter Leonidovich Kapitsa.

Eisenstein describes the solemnity of the occasion, 'together with the dons and the master, beneath the high arches soaring into the gloom of Gothic naves', an atmosphere he was later to remember when he was shooting his last film, *Ivan the Terrible*, in Alma Ata, during World War II.

At the lunch, J.J. Thomson (who had discovered the electron), turned to Eisenstein and said 'I understand that you are connected with the *kye-nee-ma*. I saw a *kye-ni-mato-graph* performance once'.

Kapitsa was a Fellow of the College. He had just been appointed the first director of the Mond Laboratory, which was funded by the Royal Society for the purposes of his research.

Eisenstein admits that he 'understood nothing' when Kapitsa showed him his laboratory, except for 'an electric machine' that was 'capable of lighting almost half of London'. This vast amount of energy 'was directed to a field of action a few millimeters in size'. Eisenstein tells us that as far as he could understand it, Kapitsa was using this machine to split particles of matter. But what caught Eisenstein's imagination was the *time* factor involved. He wasn't certain that he was accurately describing what Kapitsa was up to, but that the principle involved seemed to be that it was not dangerous to create such a vast quantity of energy, as it was only possible to do so for a very short time indeed. But nevertheless, this very brief moment was enough to study what happened, provided of course that all the necessary conditions to create such an extreme state were under rigorous control.

During his time at Trinity College, Kapitsa noted the deference shown by the students to their professors, so he set up the Kapitsa Club, which would meet each week to discuss a topic in physics. But there was a difference: this wasn't a club for the professors, but one which admitted students too, from all levels. At the start of a session Kapitsa would get things going by making an outrageously incorrect assertion. By this means, the most junior student would gain the confidence to immediately challenge a senior member of staff. There were also presentations, which Kapitsa or anyone else could interrupt at any time, with relevant points and insights, thereby creating a completely non-hierarchical forum for debate.

In 1934, Kapitsa visited his parents in the Soviet Union, but Stalin prevented his return to Cambridge. Stalin then arranged for the equipment from the Mond Laboratory to be sent to the USSR, and he set up a research institute in physics, which he appointed Kapitsa to lead. Later, during World War II, Stalin set up a Soviet atomic bomb project with which Kapitsa was involved. However Kapitsa fell out with Lavrenty Beria, the head of the NKVD Stalin had appointed to direct this vast project. So Beria complained to Stalin about Kapitsa. But Stalin made it clear to Beria that the scientists involved should be left alone to get on with their work.

Kapitsa outlived both Stalin and Beria – he died in Moscow, aged 89.

Trinity College seems to have a tradition of combining authority with challenges to it.

This tradition is still palpable as you enter the College, which was set up by Henry VIII. For example you can see his statue, above the entrance. At some point, however, someone replaced his sword with a table leg - you can still see it there today. Except when I approached the gate to the College I couldn't see it, as the space above the entrance was enclosed in scaffolding, which is why I entered through the larger entrance, away from the scaffolding. But I was told by the College porter to go out again and enter via the smaller entrance, under the scaffolding, which I duly did, to avoid tension, as I was supposed to enter through the small entrance and exit through the big exit. But when I left the College I couldn't resist making an exit through the small entrance. Fortunately I got away with it.

43. what's this?

44. time and memory

...the concept of time is based on memory, powers of recall, and association.

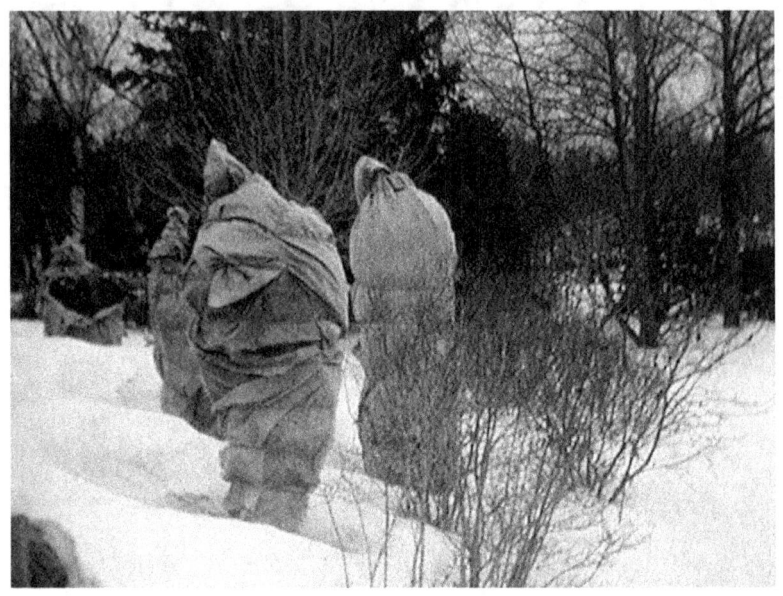

45. immigration

46. a glittering line

Noticed a big bright line of light looking down at the pond from Highgate Hill.
This line of glittering light dominated the whole pond
at that single moment in the year when the sun and the water's surface
were at just the correct angle,
and I was exactly in the right place on the hill to see that effect,
at that very instant the tiny duck was swimming past to unknowingly create it.

47. I am

I am from before all centuries.

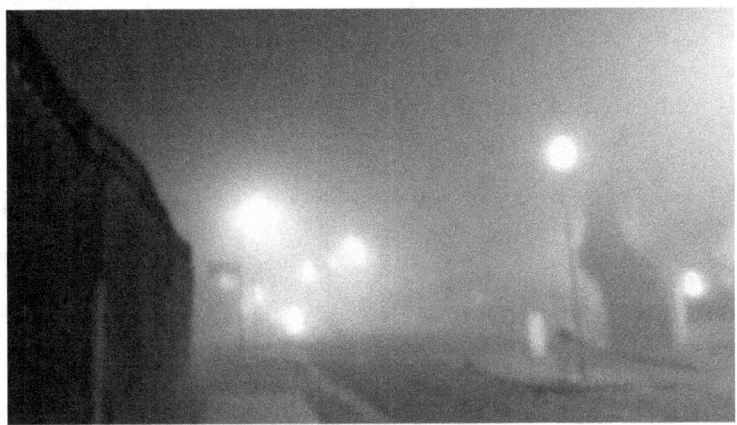

48. night, fog

49. remote interactions

   I had a great time last week, as a guest at the international School of Sound symposium at the Purcell Room on the South Bank, London. I was invited by Larry Sider, the originator and director of this extraordinary biennial gathering of filmmakers, composers, sound designers, Foley artists.

It was good to meet delegates from other countries, several of whom had read *Eisenstein on the Audiovisual*, which was a nice surprise. The new book *Cinema and the Audiovisual Imagination* was being sold at the daily bookstall.

This year the School was particularly stimulating, with the participation of the American composer Pauline Oliveros, who spoke to us via skype from Troy, just north of Albany in New York State. She got the three hundred delegates to sing, to each hum a different note, then to stand and sing out *glissandi*. Both requests produced audible sub-harmonic frequencies in the Purcell Room, reminiscent of the deep rumblings heard near giant waterfalls.

Another participant, the theatre and opera director Peter Sellars, spoke via skype from his home in Los Angeles. His very engaging talk about sound was so full of striking ideas that at times you forgot his presence - you were rapidly absorbing the new perspectives developing in front of you, before he went on to present yet another fresh and intriguing concept.

There was one delegate who stood out due to his unusual appearance. He explained to me that he was dressed in the full costume (with a four-pointed hat) of a shaman from the Sami people from northern Finland.

Ande Somby is a yoiker: he sings songs which express a distillation of the qualities of local animals, fish and insects. He told me that these songs are also used to express the nature of certain kinds of tree or plant, for example the waves in long grass stirred by the wind. He performed several yoiks, including an evocation of a wolf, with its uncannily echoing howls. Then, after a quiet moment in the song, he uttered an incredibly loud crunching sound, which made everyone jump in their seats.

The yoiks are songs in which every register of the voice is used, including overtone singing. The creature depicted in a yoik is not only expressed in terms of the sounds it makes, but its movements are also transformed into music.

50. a secret

The secret of happiness is this: let your interests be as wide as possible and let your reactions to the things and persons that interest you be as far as possible friendly rather than hostile.

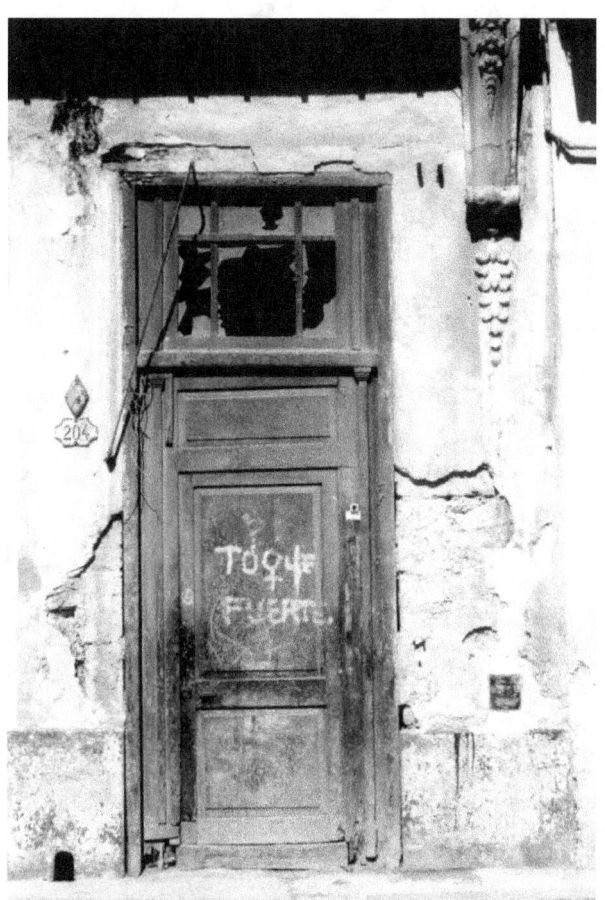

51. door of the spirits

52. what everyone likes

All my life I've had a natural resistance to whatever everyone likes, or wants, or is 'supposed' to do.

53. Minsk: a joint adventure

The grandparents of my boss were from Minsk.

As the Soviet Union was accelerating from a state-run economy towards a state of free-for-all capitalism, my boss wanted me to explore the viability of setting up an office in Minsk. There I was to meet with the director of N, a new Russian company, as this venture could only be achieved through such a collaboration. This approach to business was what the Soviet authorities called a 'joint venture' – I called it a 'joint *ad*venture'.

In Soviet times we would always travel on night trains. It was only years later that I realised that foreigners were not permitted on the daytime trains, in case they filmed or photographed 'sensitive' installations, or anything that could be of use to a potential enemy.

The first time we travelled to Leningrad from Moscow, the moonlit landscape was covered in freshly fallen snow, and we watched it, entranced, as it glided by in all its silent and abstracted forms, continually changing and evolving. And fine snow would swirl about in the powerful front light of an approaching locomotive.

For me, Russia is most itself during its all-encompassing winters, and I'd choose to go there in winter. But on one occasion I decided to go to Leningrad on the inevitable night train from Moscow, but this time in June, in the middle of the famed 'White Nights' season, when the sun hardly sets, and the night disappears.

As usual, it was dark when we left Moscow, but as we went north I was woken by a very bright light shining into our sleeping compartment: it was the sun rising at two in the morning.

Now, in the early spring, we were due to board the night train (of course), on our way to Minsk, over 400 miles away to the south-west of Moscow. We'd arrived at the big Belorussky Station, which overlooks the vast open space of Tverskaya Zastava Square. One of nine of Moscow's rail terminals, these stations provide access to an extraordinary range of diverse destinations, thousands of miles across this continent-sized country.

We looked round the cavernous waiting area, where huge numbers of people were silently and statically waiting. Spotting the Intourist booth, we waited patiently in the queue so that we could find our train in this enormous station. At last we reached the Intourist window, just in time for their employees to pull down their shutters, as if we didn't exist.

Being ignored like this was normal - we were almost used to it. But how could we find our train? No railway staff were to be seen anywhere, so what could we do? Fortunately my colleague noticed the big letters on a carriage which identified our night train to Minsk. Without difficulty we found our compartment, and as the train left, we took advantage of the tea glasses in their ornamental metal holders, that we found on our table, together with the teabags nearby, which gave us a rare warm feeling of being made welcome. All that we needed to do was to walk to the end of the very wide carriage, where there was a samovar, already filled with hot water to add to our tea in our glasses, as the birch forests began, after we'd left Moscow.

That night my dreams featured slow earthquakes, as the big carriages rolled unevenly along. In the early morning, daylight revealed the same landscape of birch forests that we'd seen on leaving Moscow the previous evening, over four hundred miles ago.

At about 6am we arrived in Minsk – at the railway station we were expecting to meet the director of N. and his colleague. Instead, as we left our train carriage we were met by two men.

In retrospect I understood how these two officials knew exactly from which end of our carriage we would emerge. This was precisely why, every time we landed in Moscow, at the start of our Soviet trips, after the usual passport and customs routines, we would have to go to the airport's Intourist booth. Here, all our reservations and travel plans, carefully organised with a specialist English travel agent in London, would be cancelled. Why? So that Intourist could draw up their own version of our trip and then give the authorities the exact details of every aspect of our itinerary. This was why the two KGB men knew in advance precisely by which door of our carriage we would leave our train: they had the numbers of our seats.

As they drove us along the multi-lane Ulitsa Lenina towards our meeting with the Director of N., one of the officials gave us a running commentary on the local industries, illustrated by various production targets and other statistics. This information wasn't that useful, as N. was a company that was primarily involved in music production and arts promotions, but it did break the silence.

We soon arrived at a decaying Sixties-style housing estate, dotted with a few worn-out skyscrapers. We left the car to go up a short flight of stairs to a flat on the ground floor of the nearest tower block, and one of the KGB officials knocked on the door. An old lady, of the *babushka* stereotype, opened the door, looked round at us and then said curtly 'Nyet, nyet, nyet', and firmly shut the door.

I can't remember what happened next, but eventually we found ourselves in a hotel room with the Director of N. and his colleague. The KGB men didn't have to be present anymore, as the hotel rooms in the hotels for foreigners were bugged anyway.

On his Soviet trips, my American boss would unlock the door to his room in the hotel in Moscow, and he would say 'Hi everyone!' to all who were invisibly listening.

After our preliminary discussions, sitting on the beds in the hotel room, the Director's colleague took us for lunch to a huge Sixties-style refectory, like in a holiday camp, with lots of glass and a rock band.

Then we were whisked round Minsk in a whirlwind tour of various hotel lobbies and artists' studios, to see contemporary paintings, of all kinds, all styles, to show us the extent of the current art scene in this city. 'Dyeep!', our host would say, with a wave in the direction of each painting: 'Dyeep!... dyeep!...dyeep!...'

Then suddenly we realise that we could miss our night train back to Moscow, so we are rushed to the station. We leap out of the car, quickly find out from which platform our train is due to leave. We dash from one platform to another, and then run across the rails in front of an incoming train, so that we can reach our platform in time, actually in time to see our carefully Intourist-booked Moscow train disappearing into the night.

As there is no waiting room in the station, we are taken to the medical emergency room. Our missed train has to be cancelled, in order for it to be possible to book seats for us on the next night train to Moscow. While extensive telephone negotiations take place in an attempt to solve our problem, dozens of soldiers are wandering around the station, dark shapes under the low-wattage lights, as in a night scene from a film set in the Second World War.

At last, in the earliest hour of the morning, another train to Moscow arrives, on which we're allowed to travel. And we leave Minsk, our train lumbering off into the deep dark of a country that no longer exists.

54. hubs

Authorities love what they call 'hubs', and they encourage them.

The hub in a wheel is the part of it that covers the least distance in its rotation.

Independent spirits are a perennial problem for hubs, as hubs immediately detect them as not being like them at all, as all hubs are obliged to remain at the centre of the wheel. The last thing they want to do is to fly around and discover things for themselves, as they aren't able to function in this way.

Obviously it's best for hubs to be fixed and firm - and at their very centre there's no movement at all, and very little diversity. This fixed and uniform centre is the attempted ideal of all authorities: everything has to be based on certainty and therefore a complete uniformity of opinion, which in itself becomes a value to uphold. Any disruption that threatens that certainty and predictability must be kept away.

I remember listening to composers who were in a position of authority: in effect they were a 'hub'. This hub was making sure that certain musicians were excluded from their (the hub's) activities, as the hub was afraid of losing its power and influence to other musicians. And the hub would spend what seemed like hours in this rather negative and sterile pursuit, which had nothing at all to do with music, but everything to do with the static power and influence of the hub.

55. aspects of education

Rewards and penalties, benefit and harm, and the law of five punishments are all secondary (or non-essential) aspects of education.

Rewards and punishments are the lowest form of education.

56. the algorithmic society

Look at any copy of *Time Out* today and you'll see 'Do This', 'Eat This', 'Drink This', 'Book This'.

These instructions bring to mind 'DRINK ME', and 'EAT ME', encountered by Alice on her arrival in Wonderland.

As Lewis Carroll tells us: 'It was all very well to say "Drink me", but the wise little Alice was not going to do that in a hurry.

'No, I'll look first,' she said, 'and see whether it's marked *"poison"* or not.'

Of course today that wouldn't happen, as we live in the digital age, the age of the computer.

But there *is* a similarity on another level: the instructions in *Time Out* are the outcome of our daily use of computer algorithms, a way of life that involves following specific instructions in a specific order, to achieve a desired effect.

Our algorithmic interaction with computers, which involves millions of people worldwide following identical paths, produces a literal society with 'how to' books and procedural paths (or 'pathways' is the fashionable term), which have only two alternatives: do it/don't do it; the correct/incorrect way of doing anything – not just with computers, but in every aspect of life.

And there has to be *one* right way of doing something, which therefore defines the other ways as being wrong. This produces a society that is based on narrow, deterministic, and literal ways of doing anything.

Extreme celebrity culture and 'selfies' are part of this phenomenon, due to instant accessibility online. But at the very root of this society, in terms of thinking, and how we approach anything, all is determined algorithmically, by a set of procedures to be followed absolutely, without question, otherwise the desired outcome won't happen.

The only choice the individual has in this context is to do something in a specified way, or not to do it – it's a computer-based, digital, binary choice.

This explains why, when someone is asked a question about a subject, the word 'so' immediately starts the answer, as 'so' is part of a deterministic pattern, which produces a specific result, as in a recipe: 'So, to boil an egg, this is what you must do': a basic algorithm, a path which you may wish to follow, or not, if you want your egg raw. In this context, grammatically the word 'so' is used to express a specific result.

In order to answer a question about global warming, you start your answer by saying 'So', as you're providing an answer according to a computer-influenced algorithm, as if you're actually facing a computer. Why? Because you're using computer algorithms all day and all night: you're on computer screens - tablets, laptops, mobile phones etc. etc. – machines in whose company you spend most of your life. But the news here is that life itself isn't necessarily an algorithm: there are multiple ways of doing the same things, there are many ways to approach subjects, to think about anything. There isn't one recipe for life. Why? Because life is too full of surprises, it is full of interesting unexpected things, it doesn't work like a computer! For this reason we should try to avoid working like a computer ourselves!

The influence of computers also explains the current obsession with the need for stories: stories are algorithmic. The obsession is always with the need for a *single* narrative, a *single* pathway, *one* algorithm at a time. But life isn't like that: it has innumerable simultaneities, innumerable stories, all of which interweave.

57. multiple approaches

It's vital for an artist to have a thick hide, especially if your work features a variety of means of expression, and you're open to using multiple approaches.

You mustn't be overwhelmed if someone is critical about your work, or if an artist deeply resents what you might say (in the politest way imaginable of course) about their work.

There should be room for diversity, and either side might change their mind at some point in the future.

58. objects on a shelf

Establishments tend by their very nature to be static.

They are often suspended in a particular period – their thinking has effectively stopped.

This is how they usually work: establishments don't normally need to think, otherwise how could they be established?

They are like a shelf on which objects, always the same ones, are displayed, immobile.

This explains their total lack of curiosity about anything else.

59. collective opinion

A wonderful phrase from Wolfgang Pauli in his correspondence with Carl Jung:

'the resistance of collective opinion.'

60. a story from World War I

He never mentioned his medals, but on one very rare occasion he summed up his wartime experiences.

His first wound was in the buttocks, called the 'coward's wound', as obviously he was facing the wrong way; his second wound was in the neck, his third wound was shrapnel in the chest - he lost a lung.

After a prolonged convalescence, the doctor approved him for his return to active service.

He protested, telling the doctor
'do you realise what you're doing? - you're sending me to a certain death'.
'What else can I do?' the doctor asked him.
'You can sign to say that I'm no longer of sound mind', he replied, 'like you did for that guy over there in that bed'.

The doctor signed his form accordingly, and that's how my grandfather survived the First World War.

61. significant funerals

Max Planck pointed out that 'science advances one funeral at a time'.

This also applies to art, and to music, and to literature, and to theatre, and to dance, and to cinema, and so on.

62. intellectuals

I don't like intellectuals because they're superficial.
They're from the top down, not the ground up.

(Appropriate for an architect, to say that)

63. melting into air – a letter from my grandfather

This was a particularly bad time for me – just before taking my final exams at university.

I must have written about this to my grandfather, who was having some struggles of his own at the Graduate School of Fine Art at the University of Pennsylvania. He'd started working there, in the Department of Architecture, at the age of 59, back in 1953.

In 1974, the architect Louis Kahn, his close friend and colleague, had recently died. Though their approaches to architecture were totally different, they would team-teach classes, and Kahn's death must have been a real setback for my grandfather. He'd succeeded him as the Paul Philippe Cret Professor of Architecture, at the age of 80.

I'd just come across his letter, written less than a year before his own death, in which he jokes that he's too young to become an emeritus professor, but that he's prepared to wait and be patient.

He sympathises with my anxieties, and at the end of his letter he writes that he sees that I'm discovering the world day by day – but that the world is probably not ready to be discovered, but lived – 'and not understanding it, is really the good reaction to it – everything changes, in a word everything transforms itself: everything is illusion – you have to take advantage of it'.

Now, forty years later, I understand better what he meant, but I still find it astonishing that he writes that 'everything is illusion', given that he was a veteran of the First World War, and that he would have lived through what I imagine would have been amongst the most un-illusory and shocking experiences a human being could have.

As a young soldier he certainly discovered the world, and didn't understand it – this war, surely one of the worst in human history, transformed everything. We are still undergoing its after-shocks today.

But perhaps our lack of comprehension is made easier to bear by the realisation that everything is an illusion – and one should take advantage of being aware of this continually transforming illusion. We can benefit from it by continually asking impossible-to-answer questions about it. What we discover along the way means that we can take advantage of this ultimately unfathomable illusion.
With its persistent transformations, it continues to always elude us. In chasing it down, we ourselves change and develop.

64. an extraordinary masterclass

I attended an extraordinary masterclass the other morning at the Royal College of Music, given by the well-known Canadian pianist Angela Hewitt. She gave guidance and encouragement to three very good pianists. Her enthusiasm, sense of humour, and perceptive comments - her singing and dancing to illustrate the points she made, succeeded in transforming academically correct performances into living, breathing music.

The vitality of contrasts was a key point, which came up again and again: contrasts in all aspects of the music. For example, the contrasts between the left hand and the right hand: 'with Bach you always practice the hands separately' she said. Other contrasts related to Mozart's melodic phrases, syncopation in Bach, and more generally, timing and its relation to breathing in and out. Also tension and relaxation: she explained about her training in ballet and in Scottish folk dance – she demonstrated several points by dancing, and also singing.

Once again I had the sense that dancing and singing are indivisible, and are fundamental elements that have to be there in some form, when playing an instrument effectively and expressively. This key factor is often neglected in the academic Western approach to music – watch audiences in classical music concerts: they tend to sit mostly completely still, like stones or blocks of wood.

Over the years I've noticed that when you are listening to some of the most powerful music of composers like Bach and Mozart, you find yourself breathing in time to it: these composers have a direct physical influence on their listeners.

As this phenomenon had never been mentioned in my musical education, afterwards I asked Angela Hewitt about it. She was enthusiastic in her response, and she again underlined the vital importance of the breath, and *how* you breathe when you perform a piece of music.

65. what is rhythm?

Rhythm is organised comparison.

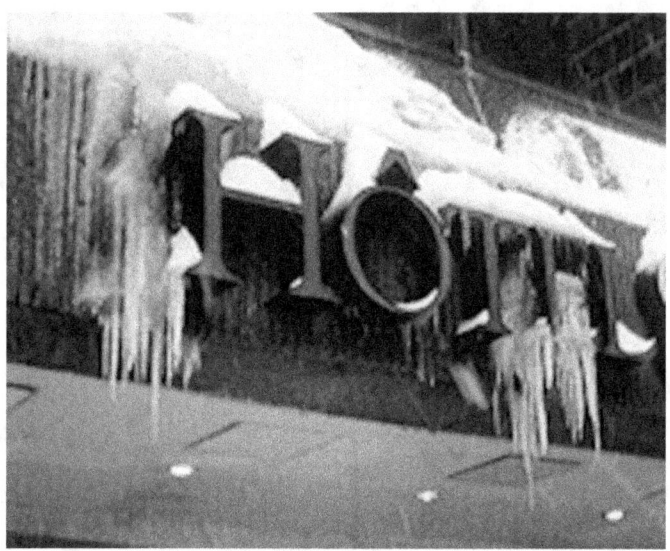

66. ice on hotel, Montreal

67. the unknown

My favourite area is the unknown.

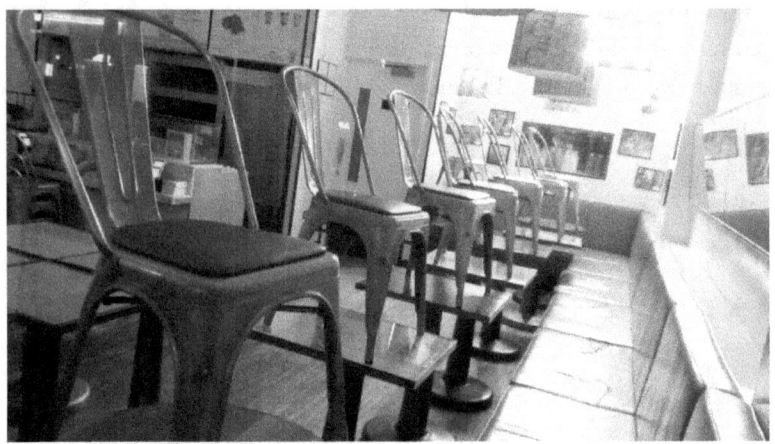

68. empty

69. open/close

Nothing lasts and nothing dies.

Nothing which is mortal is born
Nor has an end by death which comes to all
But the elements only come together
And once mixed they divide

70. writers

Many can write, some become writers.

What's the difference?

On the one hand you have the builder.

On the other hand you have the architect.

71. migration

    This concept also applies to ideas: it's no good attempting to return to a group of artists who have lived through a particular movement they have devised or in which they have participated – just as well return to live in a country you left years ago: it's no longer the same place. Most likely you'll be conceptually invisible to the inhabitants, as they will be to you.

72. frontiers

    …it is always at the frontiers that the serious incidents arise, the storms and the dramas, right on these frontiers, at the limits, that all the pathos of our sensitive existence resides.

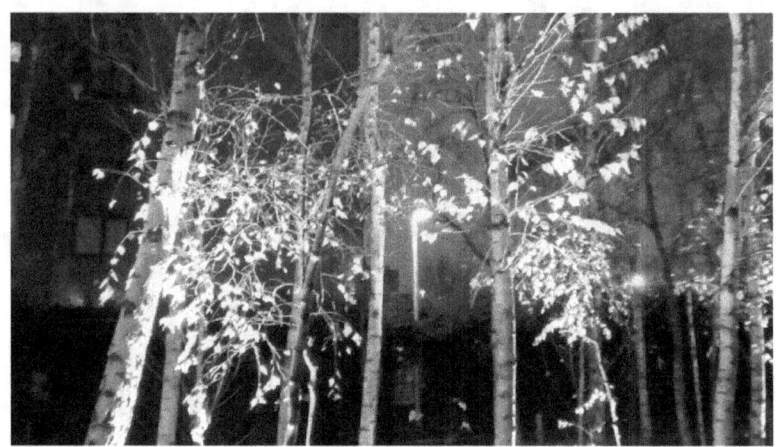

73. night trees

74. illusion, or not an illusion?

Why is it that what we see in a mirror is an illusion, when we use a mirror in a camera to split a beam of light?

Is what we see in the viewfinder an illusion too?

The teacher might answer that it's a question of degree: at one level it's reality, at another it's an illusion.

But at what point exactly does reality become illusion?

Or illusion become reality?

We haven't got all day, says the teacher, let's move on to the refractive index.

But we live continually on the borders between reality and illusion.

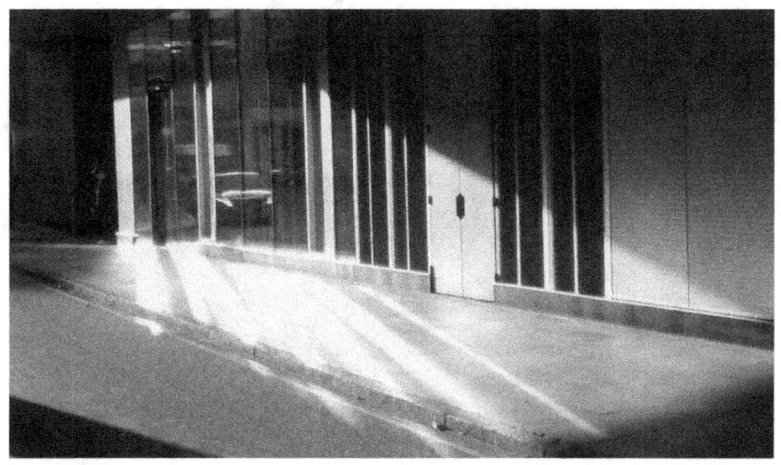

75. urban sun

76. the artist as enemy

There's a certain kind of filmmaker who really wants to make the film entirely on his own and that sort of fellow is the sworn enemy of the system.

And the system is at great pains to denigrate such a person.

They rightly regard the artist as the enemy of their profession.

77. no style

You see me here and yet I'm already changed, I'm already elsewhere. I'm never fixed and that's why I have no style.

78. unpredictability

The exciting thing about art in any medium is that it's a voyage of discovery – it's unpredictable.

Unpredictability is found in any artist who is worth discovering.

Institutions prefer this type of artist long dead.

That way such an artist is less unpredictable,

more like the institution itself.

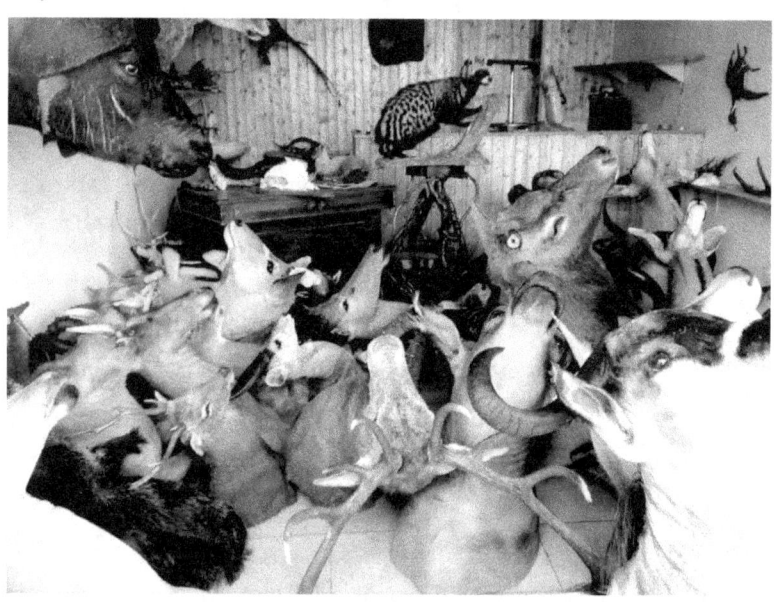

79. chaos

80. crossing

Spectacular Channel crossing the other day,

with squalls and a thunderstorm.

Wonderful changes of light,

white seabirds gliding against ash-dark thunderclouds.

End of a rainbow,

like a spectrum on the horizon,

melting in the rain on the front windows.

Heavy sea with big waves smashing against the side of the ship,

which shuddered as they broke into massive white spray five to seven storeys high.

Marvellous.

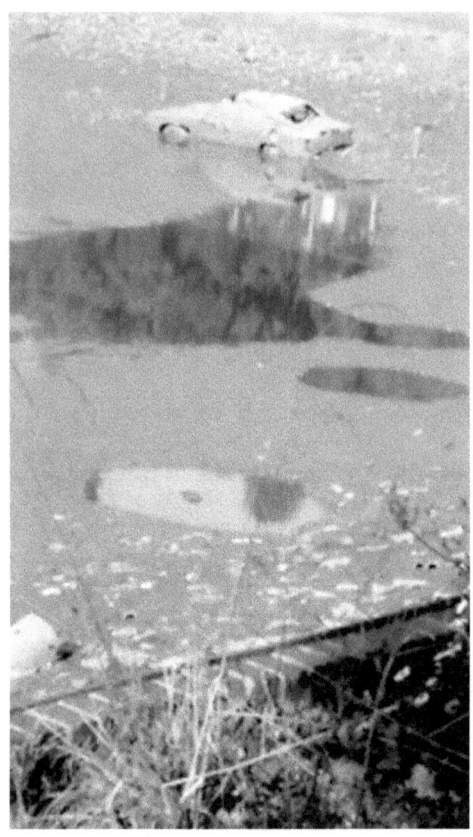

81. the dog leaps

82. unpredictable

One of the most difficult things to achieve in a work is to be successfully unpredictable.

83. authority

In the arts and the sciences, authority from above is useful, as with authority comes rejection, and rejection forces you into myriad and unpredictable directions.

This generally doesn't happen to those artists and scientists who are accepted by authority: they are in serious danger of being neutralised, through being forced to accept the inevitability of its preconceptions and cliché-ridden rail tracks, which invariably all end at the same foreseen destination, a form of death.

84. labels

Recently I've noticed a general increase in labels, in particular attached on people, often on the backs of fluorescent jackets. For example in our local supermarket I've noticed the appearance of a CUSTOMER CARE CAPTAIN. And on rail station platforms there are assortments of CUSTOMER SUPERVISORS (oddly plural, on the back of one person), and an ENGINEERING TEAM LEADER. These labels fit perfectly against posters that, like advertisements in magazines and in newspapers, increasingly feature no backgrounds at all. In some of these posters everything is so foregrounded that the advertisement becomes just a label. Even the tour guides in Oxford don't escape the label-mania: on their backs I could read GUIDE 90 MINUTES, or GUIDE TWO HOURS, and other variants.

Could this increasing foregrounding and labelling be expressing a generalised anxiety in this society, about whether someone is really doing what they are supposed to be doing – or is really what they appear to be? What is the next step here?

There could be labels on the back of other fluorescent jackets (the text is always on the back), like ARCHBISHOP OF CANTERBURY ONE MINUTE, or PRO-VICE-CHANCELLOR TWO MINUTES, or PROFESSOR OF THEORETICAL PHYSICS ONE SECOND. Or even COMPOSER/FILMMAKER FIVE TO TEN MINUTES, the latter part of the label referring to providing short introductions to works.

85. the container

The container is usually simple - it's what it contains that is complex.

86. vertical/horizontal

In the photograph you can see what looks like an ancient plinth, emerging from wild vegetation.

But we are told that you can search in vain for a beautiful statue that has been lost in the abundant undergrowth nearby.

Because, as you approach it, the plinth turns out to be a well.

If you lean over it, you can see and sense the cool air from the icy water, far below.

Amidst the dry and fierce summer heat, this hidden beauty is the only sensation that is truly refreshing.

The great changes of terrain for us consist no longer in going far away...but rather in going far in terms of depth...those are the only voyages that refresh, being the fruit of a total immobility.

87. the crocodile and the hen

One day a crocodile noticed a nicely rounded hen on the riverbank.

He approached her and was about to gobble her up, when she called out to him:

'Oh brother, don't gobble me up!'

The crocodile was so surprised by this request that he swam away, thinking that it might just be possible that the hen was right: he *could* perhaps be her brother.

But the next time he swam to that part of the river again, he'd already decided that this very appetising hen would be his next meal.

And there she was again, on the riverbank.

She could see clearly what the crocodile's intention was, so she called out to him:

'Oh brother, don't gobble me up!'

The crocodile swore at her, which gave her the time to escape his yearning jaws.

'How can I be her brother?' the crocodile, extremely annoyed, said to himself – '*she* lives on the ground, and *I* live in the water.'

As he swam home, he met his friend the lizard, and he told him what had happened with the hen.

'Don't be such an idiot!' said the lizard to the crocodile.

'Don't you know that ducks live in the water and lay eggs, and turtles also do the same thing?

And lizards like me lay eggs – and hens lay eggs, and so do crocodiles, you nincompoop!

That's why we're all related!' the lizard affirmed.

This is interesting, as some statement like the hen's plea *might* work with people in authority.

But at the very least, you need to remind them that though you might not be related, you are, more or less, of the same species.

88. America

Miami was where I first arrived in the United States, on my way to Haïti.

A bright sunny morning, alone in the big glazed atrium of the hotel, I needed bacon and eggs.

'How would you like your eggs?' I was asked.

I looked surprised at the waiter and said 'fried'.

'Sunny side up? Sunny side down? Over easy? Over medium? Over hard?'

I was totally discombobulated.

I had arrived in America.

There was no doubt about it.

89. *The Virginity of Place*

First sensations

One of the most delightful sensations I know is the sensation of waking up at a place you've never been before, but you have always wanted to see. You stretch out your arms and legs as far as you can across the huge clean cool-sheeted bed, readying yourself to receive the first, the primary sensations of the day to come, a new day, a day to be filled with the never-before-experienced, a virgin day.

For me, this is what film should be: a record of the primary sensations, capturing the freshness of the never-before-experienced at the first moment of sensation. All techniques and technology must be subservient to that momentary virginity and that direct and primal sensation of the new.

This sense of a moment which precedes discovery was evoked by the film director Bertolucci, in an interview in a documentary about Pasolini. He was asked what it had been like to assist Pasolini with *Accattone*, this poet-novelist's first film. The preparation of the first close-up, Bertolucci explained, wasn't a routine technical process, with Pasolini it was like setting up the first close-up ever.

This exciting sensation is like the instant, when after extensive research and prolonged mental digging, you have the first flash, the first glimpse of an entire work, and the sense of the definite and the inevitable which accompanies this sensation, without which the building process cannot really begin.

I had just arrived in a city I had never lived in before: Montreal. My aim was to make a film with music, a portrait of this city in the grip of a Canadian winter.

Montreal has achieved and nurtured an international reputation among filmmakers and cinephiles for being one of the key centres for film. However I was primarily curious about Montreal itself, as a place. Why is there no visual imprint of this famous city, unlike the images which cities like Paris, Rome, London or Moscow conjure up in our minds?

The sense of place

I remember hearing about a conference at a university in New Mexico. The theme was 'the sense of place', and the conference had a catchy title like *The Place of Place*. A professor from somewhere in Europe was invited, who was a specialist on names of places. He spoke with authority about the derivation of various place-names, how this process told us about the way people of different backgrounds and cultures have a diverse attitude to place, and how the concept of the place-name is directly associated with a culture's understanding of place. He also demonstrated how local stories and histories have a role in changing a space into a place. An equally well-known authority, a professor at the university where *The Place of Place* conference was being held, and whose origins were local (he was of local First Nation descent) pointed out something he had realised about his own culture, which nearly turned the European professor's contribution upside down. He informed the conference that his people had no word for place in their language at all. In addition he explained that this was the case because his people didn't travel extensively, so the idea of place wouldn't be one which they would find useful or need.

Whatever one might think about such a phenomenon, there is an example of the naming of places which in turn puts yet another perspective on this intriguing subject. Someone who had studied the origins of place-names once told me about a part of Europe where the winters are particularly severe. The strange, if not unique thing about this area is that the people change the names of their villages in the winter. So here is a case where in a sense the villages travel, but not the people. In other words, these places change so much during the winter months that the names they have in the other seasons are no longer thought to be of value to their inhabitants, or for that matter, to other people. Of course this in turn relates to why we use names at all, to the fundamental process of naming not only places, but people and things.

Nameless Places

Technological developments which mean that we can now travel thousands of miles in a matter of hours, have created the phenomenon of the nameless place. This is a personal phenomenon, related to the way in which our individual knowledge has not kept pace with the speed at which we can now be conveyed from place to place.

I experienced a disturbing example of the nameless place on a flight from London to Tokyo. For nearly eight hours we travelled over a terrain which changed very little in aspect - the seemingly unpopulated and endless wastes of Siberia. The name of this largest continuous land mass on the planet rapidly lost any meaning for me, especially as the flight wasn't crowded, the seats near mine were vacant, and I was left looking over this desolate and unchanging landscape for hour after hour. The sky was of an even grey, so the variety of weather, the changing cloudscapes and landscapes which relieve the tedium of very long flights were absent. An increasing sense of my total isolation in this expanse became stronger, as I became aware that the comforting human aspects of the landscape had disappeared. I was travelling over thousands of nameless places.

A less disturbing example of this kind of experience was on a flight over the deserts of the Middle East. I describe them in this way, as really there isn't a word to describe this undifferentiated expanse of land. I'd never flown over extensive desert before, and the weather was good. Looking down on the varied ochres, I could make out the occasional isolated cloud-topped mountain - was this one the fabled Mount Ararat? I realised that I'd only seen these expanses before in a symbolic form in atlases, with the convenient lines marking out the various countries, lines which tell you that this is Armenia, Iran, Afghanistan. The dots on the maps show us the cities, and these at least approximate the shape of a dot, but the lines are of course fictions in the desert. As a result of the loss of these, the places you see become, once again, nameless.

A more human example of this 'nameless places' experience was on a night flight from New York to Dallas. Just after taking off, I looked behind and saw Manhattan as I'd never seen it before - it looked like a complex of quartz crystals lit from within. Already at that altitude it had ceased to have a directly human aspect. This view, in sharp contrast to the human realities of this city, prepared me for what was to follow. For several hours we travelled in total darkness, except for the occasional pool of thousands of scattered dots of light, then complete darkness again, then after a while another brief pool of light, then more darkness. Though these cities were nameless to me, their brief abstractions showed the reassuring presence of the human in the encompassing and enveloping dark.

This sense of the fragility of the human presence in landscape is wonderfully expressed in some descriptions of cities, this time at ground level, where the influence of the weather creates an analogous effect.

Two cities

Lawrence Durrell, in his sequence of novels, *The Alexandria Quartet*, evokes the startling effects of a sandstorm, the *khamseen*, on the ancient city on the delta of the Nile, Alexandria. In the darkness of the storm he describes the invading sand deposited along the slats of the shutters as being like 'young snow.' A vertical wind from above seems to stir the whole city round, like in some great sandy whirlpool, as if the city were disappearing into the dunes which pre-existed it. I have never been to Alexandria, but Lawrence Durrell makes the city and its relationship to local weather and landscape so vivid, that I feel his experience is like something I might have remembered.

Dickens, in the beginning of his novel *Bleak House*, describes the dank primaeval gloom of a November day in London. Through the falling black flakes of soot from the chimneys, 'as big as full-grown snow-flakes', he imagines seeing a forty-foot dinosaur waddling up Holborn Hill. Having lived in London for the past twenty years, Charles Dickens' description is not too far from some November days there today, though the legendary fogs, the 'pea soupers' have given way to the less tangible carbon monoxide pollution from hundreds of thousands of motor vehicles.

To me it's interesting that both writers in these contexts use images relating to snow, and that both evoke the time before these ancient cities existed.

Two or three Montreals

Mies van der Rohe would have loved my day-long first visit to Montreal, during the summer: a symphony of greys.

Last April, the arrival was very different. Before the final descent the captain explained that his team would be busy on the flight deck, and would resume contact with us after landing. Below were some strange-shaped turbid clouds. Then we descended in an even grey silence. Trying to make out the first signs of the city, seconds before landing I saw just below a bas-relief of roofs of houses, white rectangles barely visible in the pale grey murk of the snowstorm. We landed on white, softly, like cotton wool.

We had arrived at a different city. The airport bus dropped us off near the hotel. To get to it, we had to climb over piles of snow by the road, in the continuing blizzard.

My third first arrival was at the end of summer. My wife and I spent our first evening on the verandah, listening to the cicadas in the trees opposite the house, in the warm night air. Again the presence of nature in the city was strongly evident. Two days later I saw a praying mantis immobile on a post in the middle of the downtown skyscraper district, in the most urban context you could wish for.

Then began the transformation of the abstract Montreal of the street maps into three dimensional moving, smelling and audible images; images interwoven with past experiences, and waking and sleeping dreams.

Our area, on Rue Sherbrooke, between the districts of Westmount and Notre-Dame-de-Grâce, reminded me of a mixture of two very different parts of London. This part of Montreal brought to mind wealthy hilly Hampstead, and at the same time the flat ambiguous spaces of South London's Balham.

From our first days we discovered the city with our feet, often getting lost and experiencing what had been unimaginable spaces on the map, with names with no meaning for us, now coming to life off the page.

We also experienced on more than one occasion a strange sensation, apparently common in those who have arrived somewhere from a distant place, and who are staying for an extended period. We quite often saw people we thought we knew in the street. This illusion was related to our animal need to find the familiar in the unfamiliar place.

North America recognized
I remember my first visits to North America, in particular New York. (Canada for me was then a place you flew over: when you could see it at all, it was just vast tracts of snow crossed by mysterious long straight lines). After the first shock of the gigantism of Manhattan, it became oddly familiar. This wasn't so much because of the countless depictions I'd seen of it in films. I realised that it was due to a much earlier experience, before I'd seen any films showing New York, or any other North American place, an early experience which could almost be considered to have become subliminal.

I grew up in France, but my French picture-books were full of North American images: huge American trucks, stripy candy Christmas walking sticks, lots of snow at Christmas, firemen in outlandish outfits, locomotives of the Old West, baseball caps. I suppose that in a country still recovering from the Second World War, it was cheaper for publishers to buy in American picture-books for children and have the small amount of text translated into French, rather than to commission these books anew.

When waiting to get my hair cut, I would read Mickey Mouse and Donald Duck cartoons. The spaces in which these characters existed were completely foreign to me, but this wasn't something which bothered me at all - it was just somewhere else, certainly not somewhere like anywhere in France. The only time I recall a problem, was when I realised that I couldn't get a candy walking-stick for Christmas, as there weren't any.

So when I stayed in New York for the first time, these huge trucks, outlandish firemen's outfits, and cartoon outlines of North American buildings had a distinctly familiar appearance. The forgotten two-dimensional images from childhood became a noisy, smelly, living and breathing reality. In my memory, the stories have completely disappeared, but the images illustrating them had remained below the surface in my mind. This is why these banal things took on (and retain) a certain dream-like quality for me.

Such things as these are intimately related to a sense of place; what makes a French street so totally different from an English street or a North American street (whether it's in a big city or a village doesn't really matter, as big cities are really agglomerations of villages). The shapes and topography of the buildings and the partitioning of space are key factors in creating a sense of place. For example there is a uniquely North American space which doesn't exist in European cities: the space between tall buildings in a block. These 'alleys' are useful as escape routes and for chase scenes in American crime films.

The topography of walls and fences is another example. I had no idea that the type of village picket fence you see in Chagall's illustrations for his book *My Life* still existed in Russia, until I saw them from the day-time Moscow to St Petersburg train. It was a surprise for me to see these villages straight out of Chagall's illustrations: previously foreigners were not permitted to travel on this route by daylight, as this was considered by the Soviet authorities to be potentially advantageous for spies.

A visit to somewhere which no longer exists
I remember my first visit to a place which no longer exists: Soviet Moscow.

The plane taxied towards a very dark terminal. After a long wait in a passport line, in a sort of electric half-light, we were propelled towards an exit. There we were faced by a slanting corridor of faces, each topped by a large *chapka*, making these dark staring figures appear taller than they really were.

On our arrival in the city we felt our way to our rooms through the underlit corridors of the Belgrade 2 hotel. A tower block opposite, The Belgrade 1 hotel, not for foreigners, was an identical twin of the Belgrade 2. I opened my 20th floor window to the blizzard; far below a huge truck was stuck, its wheels uselessly grinding the impacted snow. At last it moved a few metres, then became stuck again. The snow ploughs worked through the night. What if the power failed? There was a sense of a city on the edge of not existing, somewhere where anything could happen at any moment.

In the following days we experienced the empty full restaurants (an expanse of empty tables: 'you must book twenty-four hours in advance. We are full.'), the twelve-page imaginary menus where only *chicken tabak* was available, the total absence of cafés, then the impossibility of having a meeting with anyone, unless it was in their flat. The protracted mandatory re-booking of all travel plans inside the USSR, as if nothing had been booked already. The all-pervading sense of being controlled, monitored and observed.

The room telephone number, so you could be reached by any government official direct. The smell of Moscow: a combination of the smell of gasoline and of floor polish. The rich and dolorous sounds of the Russian language, the impassive *apparatchiks*, the numbers of people we met who had lost a relative in one of the tens of thousands of Gulags. And at night, this overwhelming Orwellian drabness created by the 40-watt lights everywhere: in offices, in shops, in houses, in the hotel, in the vast railway stations with their gigantic waiting rooms where it seemed over a thousand sombre people were sitting, waiting an empty silent time. Then there was the hauntingly repeated mournful tune on Soviet radio: *Moscow Nights*, on the night train to Leningrad. It carried in its sparse expressive notes the sense of yearning, the tragedy and pathos of a country far too vast for its inhabitants.

Rarely have I been anywhere with such an overpowering sense of place.

A Soviet Playground
Years later I visited somewhere which is the most total antithesis to a wintry Soviet Moscow: Havana. It was probably for this reason that Soviet officials considered the place such a treat, and eagerly learned Spanish to have the chance of a tour of duty there. The heat which hits you as you leave the aircraft is like the wave of heat when you open an oven door. Your body changes with this temperature, you walk differently, you think differently, you see differently as the light is so intense. For some reason the clouds seem nearer.

However I was really surprised by Havana. I hadn't been prepared to see a large-scale city which sometimes looked like a Paris transposed to the tropics, akin to the echoes of Paris, London and possibly New Orleans in Montreal. I hadn't expected the Malécon, the long curve of the treeless road by a sea wall. I hadn't expected the hideous Soviet tower blocks. In the old part of the city there is a UNESCO-protected area where occasionally the houses give up from lack of support and just collapse on their occupants. Here,

I was trying to find a way to understand my experience of this place. The most obvious ways - the music, the rum, the cigars, the heat, were already known across the globe, so these weren't really a way in to unlock the essence of this city for me. Then, as I walked down the street, I found myself looking at the doors, often in deep shadow. The doors of a particular street were astonishingly evocative. They had been re-painted numberless times, they had been weathered by hurricanes, they each were devoted to a style or mix of styles: Baroque, Neo-classical, Arabic, Belle Epoque. Sometimes they had no historical style at all, but were just a confused mass of planks just about held together, or they resembled the door to a dungeon. One was covered in metal foil, another had kept the anti-hurricane tapes crossing its window panes. The older doors had a sense of the people who had slammed them, kissed in front of them, been carried out through them - all the multitudinous important events that the families living in the houses had experienced, somehow were imprinted in the decaying textures of these doors. I noted the name of the street, and later I asked what was meant by Calle Animas. 'Street of the Souls' was the answer. Why? When was it given this extraordinary name? It was named a long time ago, nobody really knows when, I was told. Later it struck me that the 'souls' could also be translated as 'spirits'. The meaning became clearer.

I verified this meaning with another *habañero*. Yes, the spirits were, and are, the *Orishas*, the name for the Yoruban ancestor gods, whose presence in Cuba date from the colonial period.

I photographed more than two dozen of these doors. They are featured in *Doors of the Spirits*, a short music/film work: these doors were my way in to Havana.

Mysterious Montreal
On my first arrival in Montreal I bought a guidebook in the bookstore at Dorval Airport. It's called *Mysterious Montreal*. When it was too late, I realised that it featured places listed in other guides to the city, places not mysterious at all, but made to look

mysterious by photographs sepia'd by a computer graphics programme.

In London I was at the world headquarters of a bank which I hoped would transfer some money for us to Montreal, to cover our needs for the first few weeks there.

A young clerk assisted me. 'Where is Montreoor?' she asked, looking at me concerned. 'Is it in Zimbabwe?'

I tried quickly to think of something which would rapidly replace Montreal in its normal location, so we'd have some money when we needed it. I thought of Expo '67, but then I realised that this had taken place some time before she'd been born. In desperation I looked round the bank. By the wall was a real racing car, with the bank's name on it. 'Montreal in Quebec, you know, where they have the Grand Prix.'

'So you're going over with the team, are you?' she asked.

To be safe, I asked to have the details of the Montreal branch of this bank in writing.

She disappeared for quite a long time, then eventually returned with a slip of paper on which was written the address, ending with 'Montreoorrr.'

It was the first time I'd seen a name spelled with a triple 'r'.

Available Images
That story tells us more about the shortcomings of the current British educational system, than about Montreal as a place. However I am intrigued by the lack of available images which evoke the spirit of this city. The picture postcards show a stereotypical North American city, apart from the ones with the snow-bound wrought iron staircases.

Searchlights and lasers

In London you don't see searchlights panning the sky, as many of those who survived the Blitz are still around. On a very rainy night in Manhattan I saw searchlights sweeping the sky to announce the opening of a new Broadway play. So why does Montreal have a huge laser beam going round and round at night at the top of the Ville-Marie skyscraper, like a huge lighthouse in the centre of the city?

I was also intrigued by how some Montrealers seem to prefer that the Montreal winters be somehow kept a secret. Once I mentioned to my dentist the snow flurries I'd seen that morning in early October. 'Yes, but don't tell anyone about it' he said, almost jokingly.

Could it be that Montreal in the winter is no longer a little bit of London, Paris, or New Orleans? That it *really* becomes Montreal, like Lawrence Durrell's Alexandria is most characteristically itself during the *khamseen* season, or London is *really* London on a dark and damp November day? Will the equivalent of Montreal's *Doors of the Spirits* lead me to its winter?

90. to explore

To explore the world and to see what happens – the rest is vanity.

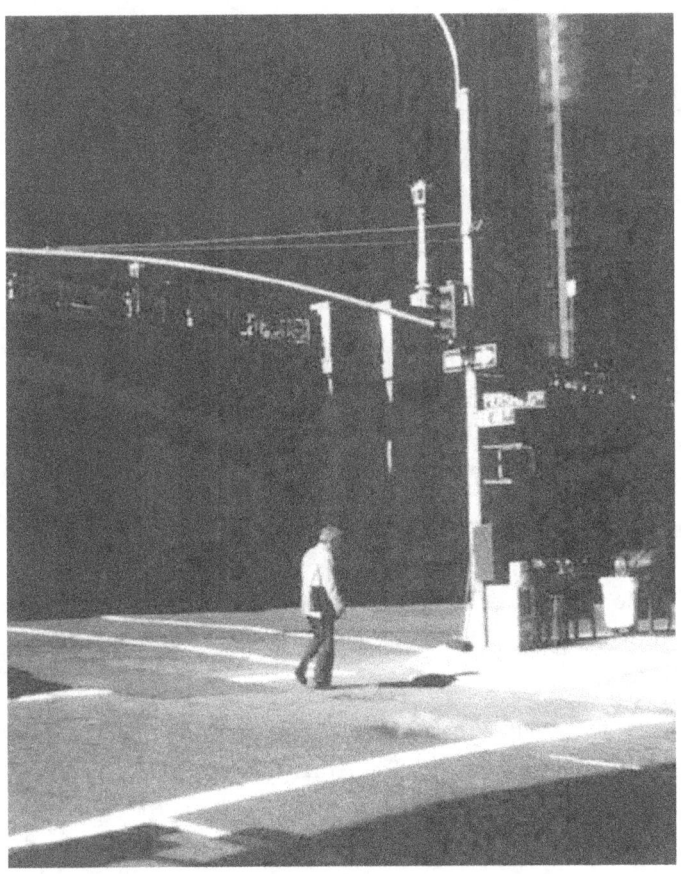

91. Manhattan morning

92. hyper-diffractive thinking

Hyper-diffractive thinking is paradoxical. It starts with a narrow space through which a single thought or idea passes, which then immediately expands into overlapping, diffracting thoughts that progress in multiple directions.

This type of thinking is often found when you use computer searches – a single thought will rapidly expand into multiple thoughts, overlapping and radiating.

This is a mental phenomenon which is often considered to result in a lack of focus, when in fact it can expand the initial thought into multiple and unforeseen directions, and therefore create new areas of focus, that are created from a single focussed thought.

This explains why hyper-diffractive thinking is associated with melancholy, or instances of depression, when thought becomes narrow and compressed. At these stages it's essential to provoke a state of hyper-diffractive thinking, by becoming aware of all sorts of sensory inputs wherever they happen to be: radio, television, computers, the cinema, theatre, dance, music. This is commonly called 'distraction', but it should be called 'diffraction', as these lines of sensory input open out into an array of different directions, prompted by the narrow space of depression through which they pass.

The melancholy which is traditionally associated with poets, for example the sixteenth century Elizabethans, is also mentioned by Rilke in his *Letters to a Young Poet*, when he notes that the most creative states are preceded by a depressed state.

It's the dynamism of multiple inputs, which are concentrated through the narrow aperture of depression, which creates irradiating and overlapping directions of ideas, impressions, and varied sequences of dynamic thought.

Hyper-diffractive thinking is also present in traditional festivals, like those for the Virgin, or other saints/gods in Spain and Italy, and in their festive counterparts in other countries and cultures: an initial single focus results in a wide variety of content and multiple references. It provokes in its narrowness a whole overlapping multitude of ideas, influences, mythical, historical and present realities.

The narrower the opening, the greater the resulting diffraction, provided that the store of initial sensory and contemplative inputs have accumulated sufficiently in the person's mind.

In Georgia O'Keefe's case, she instinctively narrowed her environs in Northern New Mexico, where she chose to settle. The result was a multiple fruition of new and original work. This also happened to Claude Monet, with the garden he devised in Giverny, a narrow focus which prompted radiating overlappings of possibilities.

93. a music/film about a city in winter

A fellow student at a film school in Canada said that my music/film of Montreal in winter didn't at all resemble the city.

On reflection, that's exactly why I made *Oserake and The River That Walks*.

The extreme winters show aspects of the modern city that would otherwise remain hidden. The heavy snow highlights colonial statues, bushes wrapped against the rigors of winter evoke images of snow-bound immigration, a hotel sign is caught in the grip of large icicles.

The severe winter, with its unstoppable forces, brings out key details from both the distant past of the city, right through to the present modern Montreal.

This is why I called this music/film *Oserake and The River That Walks*. Oserake is the surviving First Nation name of the original settlement, by the St Lawrence River, which was originally called The River That Walks, a name which itself has disappeared.

94. the point of view

The point of view of a book on Chinese art will reflect the Chinese thinking and philosophy which underlies it.

The point of view of a book on European art will reflect the European thinking and philosophy which underlies it.

What is also interesting is to look at Chinese art from a European point of view, and European art from a Chinese point of view.

This idea is applicable to any art from anywhere on the planet.

It's like exploring the possibilities of digital technology when you have been formed by ideas which preceded this revolutionary new technology.

95. Cap-Haïtien, 14th August

The clouds build up, they look grey, menacing and sag with rain. Some lightning, a few rumbles of thunder, and heavy drops fall followed by a brief downpour. Then the last rays of the day, sharp as needles through the freshly washed sky, point to bright overflows of bougainvillea tumbling over old walls.

Night. I turn into a street and find myself following a *Rara* band, in the middle of a crowd of people holding torches aflame in the darkness, dancing. I remembered the torches I'd seen in a painting of the Bois Caïman ceremony. I followed the band.

Turned with the massing crowds towards the main square. Walked past a number of halls where services are taking place: Baptist, Adventist, and other Evangelical congregations, the hymns floating into the street held aloft by the steady beat of handclaps.

With my companion I entered the cathedral facing the main square. Just inside the entrance on our left, row upon row of candles rose ablaze. She put a coin in the box at the side, picked a candle, lit it from one alight and added it to the glowing multitude. She knelt on the stone step, gazed through the iron grille at the statue of the saint flickering in the gold light of the candles, and prayed.

Bands entering the square, each with a dancing gyrating bobbing crowd in its wake. Bands with bamboo horns, bands with drums, maracas, metal beaters against metal.

Ba-dom pom, ba-dom pom, ba-dom pom, African accents driving ahead, onwards, *ba-dom pom,* against the *bom, bom, bom, bom,* the four, square, regular deep beats of the military band fixed in the square, playing European marches as varying *vaudou* rhythms form a pulsating moving circle round it.

More bands enter the square, until it seems certain that there'll be no room left, and more come along and then distant torches announce the approach of yet more bands.

Everyone plays and sings and dances at once, the square full to the brim with a mix of musics.

Cars nudge through the swirling eddies of the crowd, their horns mimicking the rhythm of the closest band.

In the distance, on the aural horizon, confused throbbing sounds, horns, and sometimes the pulse of drums. Moving nearer, sounds clarify, instruments come into focus: drum polyrhythms, maracas, individual notes on the horns. Then as the band passes and recedes, sounds fade and merge again into a confused throbbing.

Young and old dance with equal energy. Sometimes two bands confront head on, both stop and compete, until one gives in.

Ba-dom pom, ba-dom pom, ba-dom pom, ba-dom pom, ba-dom pom, ba-dom pom, ba-dom pom.

Fragments of song appearing, disappearing, approaching, receding.

An old woman possessed suddenly cries out wild variations against a repeated tune.

Each band pauses, and pays its respects to the mayor outside the town hall, at the opposite side of the square to the cathedral.

Fizzlers spray multicoloured amongst the crowd, rockets upshoot, arch and explode overhead.

The cathedral façade is pointed by lines of white light bulbs, the large central doorway shining in the darkness. Inside a perspective opens inwards, every pew is full, in front of the altar stand a dozen priests robed in white. A service of ordination is taking place, which will last nearly three hours.

Outside, excited children run about, throw fireworks, push each other into the fountain.

Bands with fast rhythms, frenetic songs, followed by bands with slow rhythms, slow songs.

Cheers, ahs and ohs follow the rapid rise of rockets, heads turning up to watch the stars bursting over the square.

The night air breathes with drums and horns.

In a pause a woman wildly intones the tune of a new song, the drums join, run into a rhythm, the chorus respond, the whistle blasts and all move off again.

Drums. Intricate patterns fit together creating flurries of notes, like horses racing, their hooves hitting the ground at different times.

Warm night full of drum pulsations, flowing improvised harmonies of songs, whistle blasts, cheers.

At last the bishop, crook in hand, emerges majestically from the cathedral, followed by a retinue of white-robed priests. The multitude in the square murmurs as the large congregation slowly pours down the steps until everyone has left the church and the square is full.

By the statue to the memory of the heroes of Independence: Macandal, Boukman and others executed in this square, the bishop stands. Before him lies an area fenced by short wooden posts decorated with sprays of *flamboyant* flowers. In the centre stands a laurel tree in full bloom with branches of laurel piled around it. Surrounding this on the ground are the arcane signs of a huge *vaudou* flour drawing. All this the bishop gravely blesses and the tree is lit.

As the first flames rise, the military band strikes up *Notre-Dame Frappez!*, the tune which traditionally accompanies the burning of the tree.

Syncopated cymbals vigorously crashing, rockets exploding, sarrusophones and euphoniums breathing a bamboo horn-style bass; the tree burns and flames rise higher and higher, incandescent ash floats down on the people who have become a single dancing mass. The tune repeats itself over and over again, becoming a vehicle for trance and possession by spirits.

Flames and sparks rise, more rockets whoosh up, fireworks swirl and flash amongst the crowd.

A white American starts dancing on his own, an excited circle of dancers form around him, a black woman dances with him, round them the people dancing and laughing.

Notre-Dame, Notre-Dame Frappez!

Amidst the dancing bodies we watch the fire relax into a glowing pile of burnt sticks and ashes; leaving the square when it is time for us to meet Michel, the master drummer.

From the main street we hear now and again faint new sounds of drums, we turn into a steep dark alleyway, go down into a tiny courtyard and face the *vaudou* temple, a small house with glassless windows, people are looking inside, craning their necks through the windows, the rattling of the drums is louder, this place is well hidden amongst the frayed buildings.

96. MIND YOUR HEAD

Corpus Christi College, Oxford, is delightfully small. I prefer it to the grand colleges, which can make you feel that really you should be wearing your Commoner's Gown and Bonnet. Here, in the small quadrangles of Corpus Christi, and its other intimate spaces like the cloisters, the golden honey colour of the sandstone contrasts beautifully with the plants and scented flowers, which are bursting out everywhere at the moment, softening the angles and straight lines of the 17th century architecture.

Apparently students at Corpus Christi are called 'corpuscles'.

In the Dining Hall, I noticed a very good portrait of a man who appeared to be meditating, his gaze directed downwards, his face a little wan. I was told that he was the founder of the College, who had died unexpectedly. Apparently his contemporaries realised that there was no portrait of him, so they commissioned a painter to depict, as best he could, the Master who had already departed this life. Fortunately the subsequent Masters of the College appear to be more lively in their portraits, which hang nearby.
I was told by a medical student (possibly a corpuscle) that the house where I was staying had been the home of Thomas Willis.

On the house there is a plaque which states that he was the Sedleian Professor of Natural Science, and had coined the term 'neurology' in his writings.

I had never heard of him – he was a 17th century doctor who pioneered the dissection of the human brain, had explored its functions, and identified diseases relating to the nervous system. One of the founders of the Royal Society, Willis knew many of the leading thinkers of his time: Robert Boyle, Christopher Wren, Isaac Newton, Robert Hooke, John Locke. Locke attended Willis' lectures as a student, and he was influenced by his ideas, including on perception.

Key sources for the explorations of Willis were the cadavers of criminals. On one occasion, with an assistant, he was opening a coffin, when the corpse inside it (of Anne Green, who had been hanged for killing her newly-born baby) emitted a gagging sound. Willis, with the help of his assistant, succeeded in bringing her back to life. It seems that this success resulted in his being appointed a Professor at Corpus Christi. This unusual path to promotion naturally aroused considerable jealousy in his colleagues.
Here was an echo of another doctor from a much more distant past: Empedocles, who had brought a woman in a coma back to everyday consciousness.

The stairs in the 17th century house which was occupied by Willis are very cramped spirals. People were smaller then, and everywhere there are labels, in big black letters on bright yellow plastic, with the modern words MIND YOUR HEAD, to prevent you being knocked out if you're in a hurry – appropriate for the house of a doctor who pioneered the study of the human brain.

97. monstrous things

It is in monstrous things that the truths most quickly come to light.

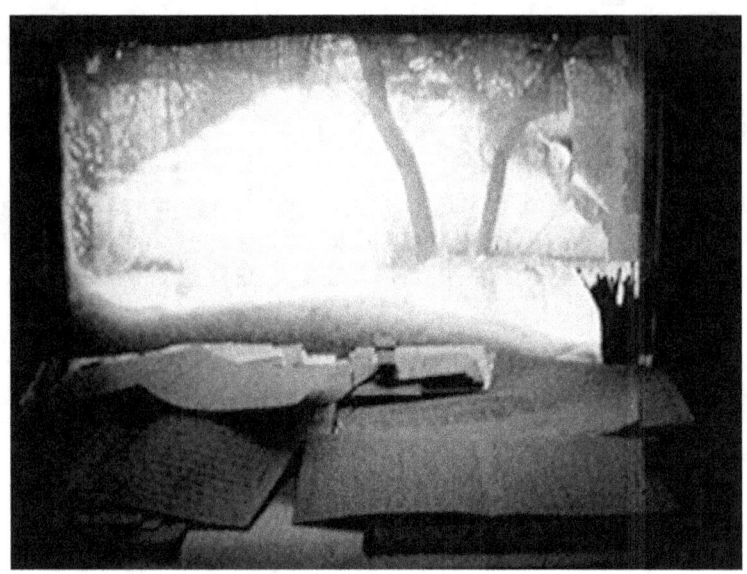

98. work-table, Montreal

99. non-linear narratives

The problem about writing, Raverat said, is that it is 'essentially linear'; it is almost impossible, in a sequential narrative, to express the way one's mind responds to an idea, a word or an experience, where, like a pebble being thrown into a pond, 'splashes in the outer air' are accompanied 'under the surface' by 'waves that follow one another into dark and forgotten corners'. Virginia Woolf replied that it is 'precisely the task of the writer to go beyond the "formal railway line of sentence" and to show how people 'feel or think or dream (…) all over the place" '.[1] The concept of tunnelling into 'caves' behind characters enfranchised her from the unwanted linear structure in which an omniscient narrator moves from points A to B. She arrived instead at a form which could 'use up everything I've ever thought'[2], giving the impression of simultaneous connections between the inner and the outer world, the past and the present, speech and silence: a form patterned like waves in a pond rather than a railway line.[3]

100. chance

I assure you that chance is also a dream.

101. the secret of a jockey's Grand National success, heard on the day of the race

Excitedly the interviewer asks the famous jockey:

'Will you be nervous once you're there at the start of the race?'

The jockey replies 'No, I'll be fine – once I'm on my horse everything flies out the window…'

102. inspiring Hockney retrospective

Had a wonderful break from the color-phobia often seen in well-behaved English art: went to the David Hockney show in London at Tate Britain.

We encounter his paintings mostly through reproductions in books, so it was striking to see them full-scale: so much attention to detail – a phenomenal evidence of hard work and care in their realisation, no effort wasted here. This level of attention to detail is combined with its opposite, a gestural freedom, and a willingness to work in a variety of styles (at times in the same work[1]) and trying out new things, an openness to new ideas.

As in the last retrospective of his work, which I saw at the same place in London back in 1988/89 [2], Hockney provides us with his own illuminating and engaging commentary in the audio-guide. His anecdotes are very amusing and feature some of the challenges he had to face: at one end of the academic scale, the threat by the Royal College of Art that he might not graduate if he didn't have evidence of a naturalistic depiction of the human body, to working in the art school arena in the 70s, when life drawing was no longer the fashion. He points out that for him drawing is a way of looking – it's a never-ending way to learn to see.

A truly diverse range of expression is shown here: explorations of colour, line, texture, space (Hockney explains that he's fanatical about space) - drawings, prints, paintings, photograph multiples, film, and most recently iPad depictions, which themselves open a new form of art, prompting new ways of creating, and looking.

His theatre work is absent - it was shown in an amazing and innovative exhibition at the Hayward Gallery in 1985.

The Four Seasons (films Hockney made from his car, fitted with nine cameras, showing composite nine-part moving images, projected on four big walls facing each other, one season on each wall) provokes an extended contemplation, with its slow hypnotic rhythm. In one of the seasons there's an amusing and unexpected appearance of a car, moving very slowly amidst the resplendent depiction of nature, shown previously without human presence. The whole work is startlingly original, not at all a diffusion of attention, which can often be the result of multi-screen work. What we are seeing is a moving image extension of his joiner photographs. Surrounded on four sides by these four seasons, filmed at the same location, we slowly move through Woldgate Woods in Yorkshire at very different times of the year, simultaneously. This experience invites a continuity of comparison, and therefore a quiet exploration of the extensive seasonal transformations of the same place.

Hockney, now 79, is asked what he would like to leave us with:
- *Joy*, he mentions above all - to develop a continuing appreciation of the wonderful in our lives and in our surroundings. Something much-needed at this time.

As a lady from Yazd explained, in the tradition of Zoroastrianism 'we wear bright colours to freshen our souls.' [2]

103. at a time

At a time when very little is happening (or seems to be happening) in terms of engagement with an audience, it's vital to realise that creativity *is* self-realisation.

The continuing creative process is directly, also simultaneously, a creation of oneself, whether an audience is there, or not.

Creativity is part of one's discovery of possibility in the world, and in one's existence, whether anyone else knows about it or not.

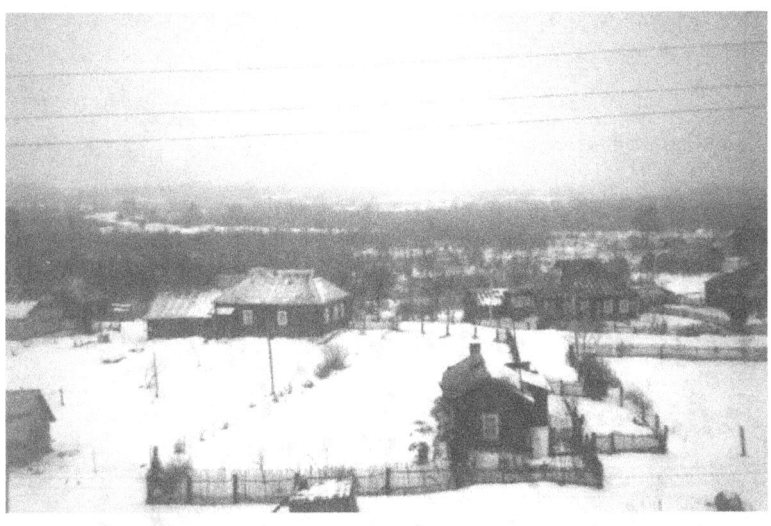

104. a village near St Petersburg

105. acceptance, rejection

It's not what others accept or reject that defines you, it's what you yourself accept or reject.

106. a different approach

After a screening of *Empedocles* I was approached by a professor who disagreed with the translation I'd used for one of the inter-title quotes from the writings of Empedocles.

Should I re-compose the music for the entire dance opera, as one specialist thinks that it's probable that there are three versions, and so at least three interpretations, of that particular text Empedocles wrote 25 centuries ago?

107. brands hatch

Noticed in a review:

'Hawksmoor is home to the Ferrari of gravies'.

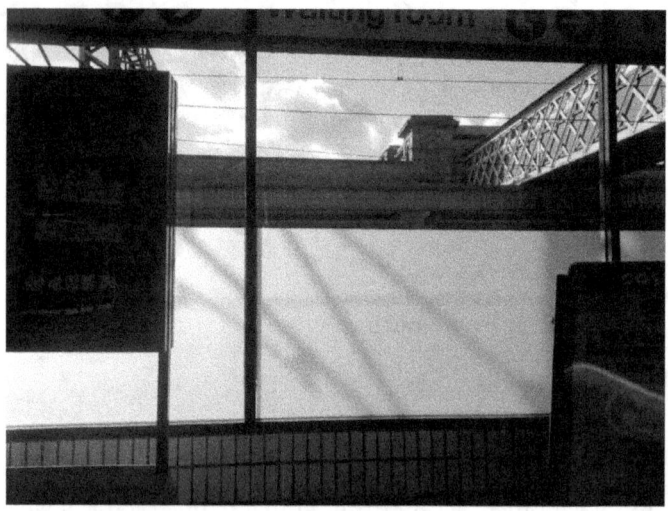

108. waiting

109. influence

　　Two huge public sculptures in the empty cemetery of an old church in central London.

There's a sign in front of them:

DO NOT CLIMB THE SCULPTURES.

I look for the name of the artist, but I can only see the name of the auction house, in capital letters.

110. the highest

　　I remember a meeting I had with the director of a well-known institution in Paris, in an office at the very top of the building, which had been specifically designed for that institution.

I said to him 'I see you have the highest office'.

He didn't find my comment at all amusing.

It reminded me of a very different meeting which was held in my hotel room high up in the formerly Soviet Intourist Hotel in Moscow.

As soon as the professor I was meeting came into the room, he rushed to see the view from the windows: never before had he seen Moscow from that height.

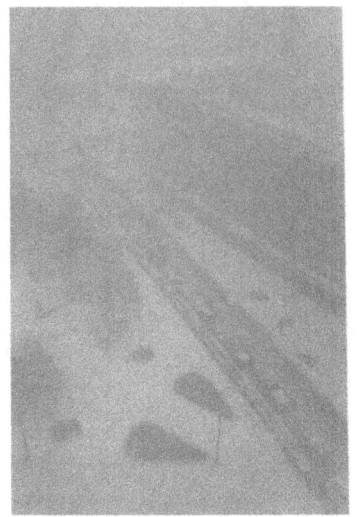 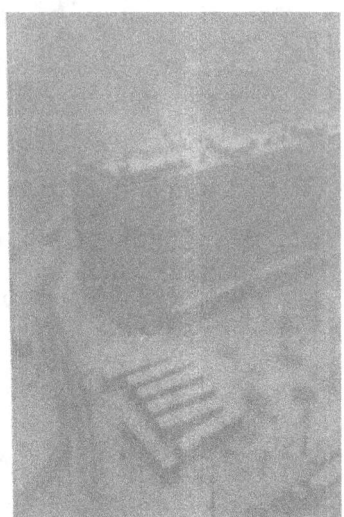

111. first arrival in Moscow

112. unpredictable art

Art in any medium only works if it's unpredictable.

If on the first encounter it's predictable, then there's no space for you to interact with it.

It becomes monolithic, like a brick wall.

Brick walls can become interesting when they are on the edge of chaos.

113. the Jarman Building

Just finished teaching a course on the audiovisual in cinema, at the University of Kent's School of Arts, an extension of the course I taught at the BFI last year.

The School of Arts is in the Jarman Building, a hyper-modern structure with massive windows at the front. Inside these windows are blinds, which on the outside diffuse the sunlight in a mobile silver glow, which accompanies you as you walk by.

Inside there are vermilion-coloured sofas, a little like in the space station in Stanley Kubrick's *2001, A Space Odyssey*, with rows of cubicles for the staff, reminiscent of the monasteries at the origin of universities in Europe. These traditions are deeply anchored - I've also seen these rows at Columbia, at Princeton, the University of Southern California in Los Angeles, and Texas Southern Methodist University in Dallas. And of course in the older colleges at Oxford and Cambridge, which really were like monasteries.

The campus at Kent is most attractive. It spreads out spaciously on the hill that overlooks Canterbury with its medieval inns, the famous cathedral, and the ancient town gate through which the double-decker buses inch their way at their maximum slowest speed each day.

114. perfection

There are pictures that become so hackneyed through reproductions that it is impossible to look at the originals. Such is the fate of almost everything in the National Gallery in London (...) where *chef d'oeuvres*, too perfected and finely finished, are reproduced in 'long shot' and described boringly, dryly, and unintelligibly.

115. identity crisis

Ultimately the process of exclusion can lead to the disappearance of the excluder.

A village which doesn't accept new blood, new arrivals, is contributing actively to its own dissolution - openness to change and the evolutions which result, are inevitably inter-dependent.

116. foreign

Culture has always been an import. Very seldom has culture ever sprung from the ground by way of a native.

117. *Ways of Knowing*
Knowledge, Information and Value

> *He who knows what it is that Heaven does, and knows what it is that man does, has reached the peak. Knowing what it is that Heaven does, he lives with Heaven. Knowing what it is that man does, he uses the knowledge of what he knows to help out the knowledge of what he doesn't know.*
>
> *Chuang Tzu,* The Great and Venerable Teacher

Is knowledge information plus a sense of value? Could one even say that the gap between information and knowledge is one of the flash-points of creativity?

These questions are too abstract for me. In order to try to understand them I need an immediate plunge into the material, the tangible. Perhaps the following examples will help. I've decided to limit my investigation of the subject to various figures around Lawrence Durrell's *Alexandria Quartet*. Later I allow myself one or two digressions.

Larry and Huw
I remember Huw Wheldon as the deeply serious, occasionally challenging interviewer on BBC Television's *Monitor* arts programmes during the Sixties. Lawrence Durrell's reputation had been established by the success of his *Alexandria Quartet*, he became a 'must-have' on Wheldon's interview list. So it was that he went to Provence to interview Larry Durrell for the *Monitor* programme. Things did not go well.

Early in the first session Wheldon had contradicted Larry, telling him, 'You don't realize what you've written.' Larry had stiffened. In Nîmes the next day, on the steps inside the magnificent Roman amphitheatre, Larry got his own back. He cornered Wheldon on Taoism, asking whether the Monitor *programme's star knew Chuang Tzu. 'No', said Wheldon curtly. Larry enlightened him: 'A philosophic comedian, a sort of hidden joke. He's really the basis of early Chinese religion.' When Wheldon quoted Pursewarden to Larry - 'The thing to do is to laugh until you hurt, and hurt until you laugh' - Larry replied, 'Yes. You have to,' adding pointedly, 'Yes - and you?...If you want to be a human being, you'd better learn.'* [1]

Looking more closely to see how this clash came about, it's evident that it was Wheldon who lit the fuse. When he tells Durrell *You don't realize what you've written,* in effect he is saying that the writer is not only naïve, but that he wasn't even aware of what he was doing when he was writing the *Alexandria Quartet.* In other words, he was just transmitting information without really being conscious of its real meaning or value, like a computer at an airport that processes flight information without understanding the value of what it is doing or the significance of the destinations it is displaying. In a sense, Wheldon was telling Durrell that he was a little bit ignorant, certainly not as self-aware or knowledgeable as *he* (Huw Wheldon) was.

This is why Durrell was able the next day to get his revenge, through *knowledge.*

But it's the nature of this particular knowledge which provides Durrell's *coup de grâce.* Chuang Tzu often used humour to transmit his ideas. The resulting inner laugh or smile isn't just pleasurable, it's also memorable. And humour can be a powerful distance-creating mechanism - it enables you to see an unforeseen side to something you thought you knew. So Durrell scores on several fronts: he can take pleasure in Wheldon's reluctant acceptance of his own complete ignorance of Chuang Tzu, as well as enjoy telling him in a jokey sort of way how fundamentally important this philosopher was. After all, how could an educated man like Wheldon be unaware of such a valuable and hugely influential thinker? But without information there can be no knowledge, and without knowledge there can be no humour. So when Wheldon humourlessly tackles Durrell on the subject of humour and its philosophical importance (which Wheldon evidently doesn't share) Durrell has the ideal opportunity to triumphantly twist the knife he'd plunged in earlier. His remark makes Wheldon's insulting comment the previous day pale into insignificance.

Not only does he treat Wheldon as if he's a child, but he accuses him of not being human, and humour does appear to be one of the characteristics which differentiate humans from other animals. A sense of humour enables us to laugh at others (as Durrell is doing here) but also to laugh at ourselves. It's a characteristic which implies a degree of self-knowledge, something else that Durrell is implying Wheldon doesn't have.

Durrell and Bronowski
Very different was Durrell's encounter with another great televisual presenter, Jacob Bronowski, who later became known for *The Ascent of Man*, his inspiring series of television programmes and subsequent book. (*The Ascent of Man* was commissioned by David Attenborough, when Huw Wheldon was Managing Director of the BBC).

Because Durrell in previous interviews had mentioned that Einstein's Relativity theories had been a key influence on him in the composition of *The Alexandria Quartet*, it was most likely for this reason that Bronowski wanted to interview him in 1961, for a BBC

programme about the relationship between science and literature. The subject of other writers came up during the interview, more specifically their quest for a new form. Durrell explained that
...other writers hadn't expressed what I think Einstein would call the 'discontinuity' of our existence, in the sense that we no longer live (if his reality is right) serially, historically, from youth to middle age, to death; but in every second of our lives is packed, in capsule form, a sort of summation of the whole'.[2]

Here we see the fusion of two types of knowledge: scientific and experiential. Though Bronowski, at the conclusion of his *Ascent of Man*, points out that 'science is only a Latin word for knowledge', he knows that human knowledge has grown into multiple and separate paths. His book is a brave attempt through a historical overview to overcome the current limitations of extreme specialisation in Western science. He also believes that a sense of value, even an ethical sense, is inherent in knowledge:

Knowledge is not a loose-leaf notebook of facts. Above all, it is a responsibility for the integrity of what we are, primarily of what we are as ethical creatures (...) Knowledge is our destiny. Self-knowledge, at last bringing together the experience of the arts and the explanations of science, waits ahead of us.[3]

This thinking provides a direct bridge to a writer like Durrell, who was influenced by both the scientific knowledge of his time, and by other writers and artists. The 'capsule' idea that he described to Bronowski is a good example of such a hybrid thought, and one made possible by his own experience and self-knowledge. I feel that it is of value, as I think that it shows us a completely new way of apprehending the passing of time in our lives: time is more akin to something one can perceive at different levels of magnification under a microscope. Whereas the world of information and its transmittal can be instant, as it is today, the world of knowledge has to have time for it to exist at all. Time is also inherent in Bronowski's view of knowledge - it is 'destiny', and it 'waits ahead of us.' Knowledge is a living and breathing dynamic force. Perhaps Durrell's wonderful concept also has its roots in another writer, a poet, who was also a powerful influence on him, both when Durrell lived in Alexandria, and when he was writing the *Quartet*. This Greek poet, a lifetime resident of Alexandria, was Constantine P. Cavafy.

Cavafy, Knowledge and Memory

In his poem *Ithaka*, Cavafy addresses Odysseus. The poet hopes that as Odysseus sets out to return to Ithaka, where he ruled as king, that his journey will be long, with many adventures and discoveries. Cavafy tells Odysseus that without Ithaka he would never have set out to return there, as his extraordinary journey turns out to be his destiny. Ithaka has never fooled him - if he finds her poor, now she no longer has anything left to give him, as by then he'll have understood the meaning of these Ithakas.[4]

Though addressed to Odysseus, this poem is really aimed at us all. Time is a key element in the poem, and it is intimately associated with space, creating a long journey of discovery, with the gradual acquisition of knowledge and experience over time. However, the memory of Ithaka represents for the traveller an understanding of knowledge itself. Ithaka is not only a destination, and a destiny, but it's also the place from where Odysseus set off. Ithaka is an entity which cannot exist apart from the journey, and one which can only make sense once this journey is complete. It's an image of birth and death, where only the completeness of death can enable the understanding of a life.

For Cavafy, Alexandria was an Ithaka: he never really left it, but travelled instead in time and memory. His Alexandrian spleen is eloquently expressed in his poem *The City*. He says that he'll leave to go to another shore, another country, to find a city which is better than Alexandria. But whatever he tries to do, his fate determines that it turns out wrong. He asks how long he can allow his mind to decay in the city in which he has spent his ruined and wasted life. Despite his yearning to leave, he knows that this city will always pursue him: he won't find somewhere new, but he'll grow old and grey in its houses, its districts. He'll always end up there, as no ship or road can provide him with an escape to a better life. As he's wasted his life in his city, in a small corner of the world, he has thus destroyed his life everywhere.[5]

Cavafy solved his problem with his city by turning it upside down. Transforming information into knowledge, he shook out of Alexandria the multiple layers of its Graeco-Roman past, and combined them with his most personal experiences. He created a new city which became *Cavafy's* Alexandria, instead of indulging in his earlier depression, caused by the separate facts of Cavafy *and* Alexandria. He made his knowledge of Alexandria's ancient past come alive in his poems and in his conversation, so that his visitors sometimes had the impression that he was conveying gossip about people he knew in the city, and not those who had lived there centuries ago.

Cavafy never bothered to have electricity installed in his flat. For visitors who wished to see him because they'd heard of his work (even though he was hardly published in his lifetime) the poet had an intriguing value system. If he found a visitor boring, he'd only light one candle; he lit several for those who interested him.

E.M. Forster was an admirer and a visitor, and he understood *The City* when the poet read it to him in Greek. Cavafy became ecstatic and 'lit candle after candle until the room blazed with light.'[6]

> *...the Alexandrian Greek poet Constantine Cavafy...became a great influence. I'd read* The City, *which impressed me. I read more of his poems and I was so struck by their directness and simplicity; and then I found the John Mavrogordato translation in the library in Bradford... that summer, and I stole it...I don't feel bad now because it's been redone, but you couldn't buy it then, it was completely out of print. Mind you, in the library in Bradford you*

had to ask for that book, it was never on the shelves. If you had the intelligence to look it up in the catalogue and ask for it, then it would be all right. But if you were just a casual person who took it down off the shelves and read one of the poems, well it might be too wicked and you might go home and jerk off with poetry.[7]

David Hockney and Received Ideas

Perhaps for a brief moment you thought that the above quote was from E.M. Forster.

Actually it's from David Hockney:

...the Alexandrian Greek poet Constantine Cavafy...became a great influence. I'd read (Lawrence Durrell's novels The Alexandria Quartet; *in the back of* Justine *there's Cavafy's)* The City, *which impressed me.*

I left the bracketed bit out of the original quote to create the feeling of surprise you experience when you come across something which isn't what you first thought it was. The exploding of a received idea is something which works in this way. In a sense the received idea represents the line of least resistance in thought, an idea which may have had a modicum of truth in it once. It's normally associated with an easy idea which is shared by a significant number of people, something exposed so wittily by Flaubert in his *Dictionnaire des idées reçues*, a collection of absurdly habitual thoughts.

It's interesting that David Hockney found his visit to Alexandria a disappointment (after all Cavafy himself wasn't really taken by his home town at first) – Hockney explains how one never really believes how places can change: when he went to Alexandria he thought that he'd find Cavafy's city.[8]

In order to capture what he felt was the atmosphere of Cavafy's Alexandria for his set of Cavafy-inspired prints, he had to visit Beirut. Here he had found a cosmopolitan city, with French and Arabic inhabitants, but not many Greeks.[9]

Alexandria in Hockney's imagination had become a received idea.

The city had moved on, both from the perceptions of it Hockney had gleaned from Cavafy, as well as from Durrell's later evocation of the city. In order to give his Cavafy prints the primacy of lived experience, Hockney had to find a city that he felt came close to Cavafy's Alexandria: Beirut.

A received idea is knowledge in an arrested state of development. It goes back to being information, except that it has now become information which is inaccurate or simply dated and mostly irrelevant, something without value. If you accept that value is something which is useful or gives pleasure (or both) to the recipient, then information becomes knowledge when it has value to the recipient. However it's interesting that a moral and ethical dimension is absent from this definition of value, and consequently absent from this description of the nature of knowledge and information. For example, a received or incorrect idea may be considered to be valuable by the person making use of it. I'd like to return to this point later.

In search of more knowledge, Hockney pursued his Cavafy-inspired vision by visiting John Mavrogordato, who had made the first English translations of the poet. This proved to be a strange visit, considering the importance of memory in Cavafy's work.

Hockney traced him to a house in London. The translator was very old, and his wife explained that Hockney must get anything he needed from her husband in writing, as he had a really bad memory. This turned out to be an understatement, as his memory was so bad he'd forget what he'd said at the beginning of his sentences, forget who Hockney was, and what he was doing there. Hockney would try to explain to him again what he wanted to know, but he realised that it was a hopeless situation.[10]
Without time there is no knowledge, so knowledge is also impossible without memory.

Kerby (After Hogarth) Useful Knowledge

Hockney painted *Kerby (After Hogarth) Useful Knowledge* after doing research for creating the sets for Stravinsky's opera *The Rake's Progress*. He had come across an etching by Hogarth, a frontispiece to a textbook on perspective, *Dr Brook Taylor's Methods of Perspective*, published by Joshua Kerby in 1754. This crowded picture was a demonstration of the absurdity of various errors of perspective:

You could see what it was about, how Hogarth meant it: if you did not know the rules of perspective, ghastly errors like this would occur. But I was attracted to what Hogarth thought were the errors and I thought I also saw that they created space just as well, if not better, than the correct perspective he was praising.[11]

Through a demonstration of errors, Hockney had discovered that Renaissance fixed point perspective is a received idea, somewhat like the fixed point serial, historical progress from youth to middle age, to death, mentioned earlier, which Durrell wished to overturn in *The Alexandria Quartet*. Hockney explains that

...space and time were considered separate and absolutes - they always existed. Einstein said, This is not the case, they're not absolutes and they depend a great deal upon the observer; different observers see different events at different times.[12]

Hockney experimented with some of the perspectival errors in Hogarth's print, especially using reverse and multiple perspective. Particularly striking are his reverse perspective chairs, which he achieved both in painting and in photography, and his multiple perspective photographic collages, now realised in painting in his *Grand Canyon* series.

The Chinese Scrolls

A chance visit to China enabled Hockney to overcome his received ideas about Chinese art:

When I went I knew very little about Chinese art. I discussed it a little with Stephen Spender, who was saying, Isn't it all a bit the same? And I said, It seems to be. These are the words of the ignorant, frankly.[13]

Hockney's awareness of his own ignorance opened the door to a type of visual thought, a visual knowledge, new to him in painting. He demonstrates this in his film *A Day on the Grand Canal with the Emperor of China, Or Surface is Illusion, but So is Depth*. Here he shows us (with a fixed point perspective painting by Canaletto hung behind him) a Chinese scroll, gradually unrolling it, so that we can experience it in the way the artist(s) intended. He shows us portraits of Chinese cities, full of the most extraordinary detail, because, as he explains, the artist enables us to see round corners, and behind walls. In retrospect we have seen this level of detail before: in Hogarth's list of perspective errors.

Then Hockney shows us a later Chinese scroll which has been influenced by Renaissance fixed point perspective. It has much less detail, and Hockney notices that it's easier to find the painting of the Emperor in it, as he's separated from his fellow-humans; he's not shown amongst his subjects in the same way as in the older, multiple perspective scroll. He goes further and points out that monotheism is related to the fixed point perspective, whereas the Chinese absence of a single god appears to encourage multiple perspectives. Hockney concludes that the artist's use of perspective isn't just a visual trick, an optical illusion to create space on a two-dimensional surface, but that it is a whole way of perceiving the world. It shows knowledge in an ethical and moral dimension, far beyond the knowledge of technique as technical information: it's a way of knowing the world.

De Kooning and Optical Illusion

In the late '70s I came across another awareness of illusion which caught my imagination. It's related to the idea of optical illusion, a form of visual information we receive which is not what it appears to be, a sort of received idea of the eye and brain.

This interesting view of illusion came up when Harold Rosenberg was interviewing Willem de Kooning. I enjoy the unplanned moment which can happen in interviews, when the interviewee says something so 'off the wall' that it throws the interviewer's planned questions out of the window. De Kooning and Rosenberg are discussing optical illusions, and the artist describes a diagram that he has seen: two parallel lines are superimposed on an array of lines which makes the two lines appear to be narrower at the centre, and so they no longer appear to be parallel. For de Kooning this is not an optical illusion, as that is exactly how one sees these two lines. But Rosenberg objects – he says that if you measured the two lines they would turn out actually to be parallel, and that is why it must be an illusion when they don't appear to be so. However, for de Kooning this traditional explanation isn't satisfactory:

De K: But in a painting, that's the most marvellous thing you can do. That's the very strength of painting, that you can do that. It is "optic" naturally, because you have to have eyes to see it. All painting is optic. If you close your eyes you don't see it. But if you open your eyes with your brain, and you know a lot about painting, then the optical illusion isn't an optical illusion. That's the way you see it.
R: The way you see something doesn't mean necessarily that that's the way it is (...)
Putting a stick in water so that it looks as if it's broken...
De K: Well it is. That's the way you see it.
R: What do you mean, it is broken? If you pull it out of the water it's not broken.
De K: I know. But it's broken while it's in the water.

R   *The break is an illusion...*
De K: *That's what I'm saying. All painting is an illusion. Mondrian gives you one kind of illusion, whatever you call it, tension...he calls it "dynamic equilibrium", or "clear plasticity". I don't care what he calls it. That's the way you see it.*[14]

Here we are witnessing the clash of two completely different ways of knowing. Rosenberg's way is based on plausible information he has been taught, which he has accepted, whereas de Kooning's way is based on decades of experimenting with multiple levels of abstraction and representation in his work. He knows the difference between visual information and scientific information, that there is more than one way of interpreting and knowing the visual, that there are multiple forms of knowledge. This is the difference between an artist and most critics, between the 'hands-on' knowledge gained from a creative process, and the received ideas of others.

Nabokov's Lying Butterfly

De Kooning's inspired statement that a stick is *broken while it's in the water*, leads me to an area which appears to border on the miraculous. It involves a complex visual illusion found in a discrete corner of the insect world. It provides a living proof of de Kooning's idea of an illusion, which at the same time is not an illusion. It's also an example of knowledge which perhaps isn't knowledge (in the way we have understood it so far) and of a sense of value that is beyond the human.

The novelist-lepidopterist Vladimir Nabokov had a passionate interest in mimicry and disguise in the animal world. In 1941 he wrote a lecture/essay where he mentions

...a species of butterfly on the hind wing of which a large eyespot imitates a drop of liquid with such uncanny perfection that a line which crosses the wing is slightly displaced at the exact stretch where it passes through - better say under - the spot: this part of the line seems shifted by refraction, as it would if a real globular drop had been there and we were looking through it at the pattern of the wing.[15]

This is a description of an illusion of an illusion, a trompe l'oeil of refraction.

To get a sense of what Nabokov was describing, I looked in an encyclopaedia I have which shows photographs of over a thousand butterflies from around the world.[16] Though I didn't find the species he refers to, I noticed that many species have eyespots which mimic the reflection of a light on the surface of a real eye, what lepidopterists call 'pupilled' eyespots. However I did find a species which carries this mimicry to a further level of sophistication. The *Mesosemia* genus from South America has three different-sized reflections of light in the eyespot, creating the illusion of a glistening convex eye. This type of sophistication (as Nabokov points out in *My Father's Butterflies*)[17] is actually beyond the useful, it's a sort of mysterious joke played on us by nature. This is why now I'll turn away from these extremes to return to the human world where the concepts of information, knowledge and value can reappear.

A Mosaic Floor in Grado

A few years ago I was in Italy, visiting an early Christian cathedral in Grado, a little seaside town in the province of Friuli, during a summer trip. When my eyes had got used to the initial darkness in the building, I could make out a complex mosaic on the floor in front of the altar, representing the town of Grado almost surrounded (as it is) by the sea. In the middle was a bird's eye view of the town, but looking more closely you could make out that the sea around it was shown in a series of sections, each of a slightly different colour and design. It was as if the artist(s) had taken photographs of the sea, a series of snapshots which had been assembled in a filmic sequence of mosaic "shots," around the depiction of the town, evoking the multiple states of the surrounding and extensive expanse of water.

Recently I found out that this cathedral dates from the 570s, and that the town could barely afford the building of it, let alone pay for the mosaic floor. For this reason this mosaic had been created over an extended period, paid for by more than twenty named donors, when the money was available, and realised by the square or linear foot - a mosaic by subscription.[18]

In this bird's eye view, the borders of the sections showing Grado disappear, as Grado was and is, an easily defined set of visual details. Amidst the busy mass of largely straight lines and static textures of the townscape, the artist(s) could easily hide the straight lines of the section edges. But the continually moving sea presented them with an insurmountable problem. An extensive and encompassing surface which is mobile and continuously changing isn't so readily defined, so the edges of the sections created at different times are much more visible.

You could say that my cinematic impression has been made valueless by the factual reason for the appearance of this mosaic, that my concept is based on an illusion.[19] You could also say that Nabokov's moth isn't that interesting because it just imitates something banal like a water droplet on a leaf. Or you could point out that de Kooning was wrong about the refractive index and optical illusion. But this would cast aside such things as the wonderful meeting between Cavafy and E.M. Forster, and Hockney's comments on Chinese landscape painting. You would be left with Huw Wheldon and Lawrence Durrell, a point where information never made it to knowledge, as Wheldon's sense of value was not there to make a significant way of knowing possible for him.

During this brief investigation into ways of knowing, it's become apparent that the relationships between information, knowledge and value form a complex web of perspectives, affected by a multitude of factors. Similar ideas come up in the most diverse situations, paradoxically highlighting the importance of individual experience. There are also the wider factors involving memory and history, time and acculturation. Then there is the area involving received ideas, and errors (both real and apparent) which appear to be one of the key sources of creativity. And there are the areas where the concepts of information, knowledge and value cease to have relevance, as you are dealing with what is at present unknowable.

For my part, I shall now use the Grado mosaic idea to attempt to solve a compositional problem I've had in a music/film work in progress.

1   MacNiven, S, *Lawrence Durrell, a Biography*, Faber and Faber, London, 1998, p.512.
2   Ibid. p.514.
3   Bronowski, Jacob, *The Ascent of Man*, BBC, London, 1976, p.436.
4   In *Cavafy, Constantine, Selected Poems*, trs Edmund Keeley and Philip Sherrard, Princeton University Press, 1972.
5   Ibid.
6   MacNiven, S, *Lawrence Durrell, a Biography*, p.267.
7   *David Hockney by David Hockney, My Early Years*, Thames and Hudson, London, 1988, p.63.
8   Ibid. p.89.
9   Ibid. p.102.
10 Ibid. p.102.
11 Hockney, David, *That's the Way I See It*, Thames and Hudson, London, 1999, pp.29-30.
12 Ibid. pp.125-126.
13 Ibid. p.78.
14 Rosenberg, Harold, *Interview with Willem de Kooning*, in Arts Council exhibition catalogue, London, 1977.
15 In *Atlantic Monthly*, April 2000, p.62.
16 Feltwell, John, *The Encyclopedia of Butterflies*, Quarto Publishing plc, London, 1993.
17. *Atlantic Monthly*, April 2000, p.68
18 Lowden, John, *Early Christian & Byzantine Art*, Phaidon Press, London, 1997, p.142.

19 Later, I found out that the mosaic I describe here was actually made much more recently, in 1950.

But I still like its photographic shot approach to the mosaic representation of the sea.

I was under the illusion that it was an early Christian work, but the knowledge of my error doesn't take away its optically inventive approach, which caught my imagination at the time, and which consequently prompted my memory of it when I wrote this text.

118. *Diversions*

The other day I came across this thought about stories, from Primo Levi. (Today we're told that everything must have a story - this is probably related to the obsession with brands). Anyway, this is what Primo Levi pointed out:

'... the more interpretations a story can give, the more ambiguous it is... a story must be ambiguous or else it is a news story, therefore everything is valid, rationality is valid, the science-fiction world is valid, and even the sensation of dreams is valid.'

This idea certainly applies to the ambiguities in *Diversions*, a stream-of-consciousness music/film.

119. illusions of illusions

Things themselves are lying, and so are their images.

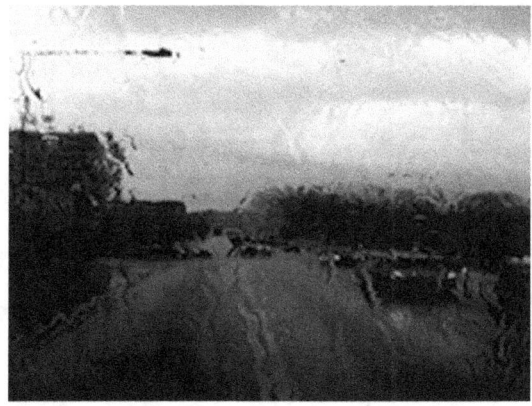

120. London rain

121. *Machines*

In one aspect our digital age can be compared to that distant time of my favourite Early Greek philosophers (one of whom I celebrated in my dance opera *Empedocles*).

In those days ideas were transmitted by speeches and discussions, like today.

However, for the future, these ideas were set down in rolled parchments (of course publishers didn't exist at that time), which is probably why only fragments from this wonderful early philosophy have survived.

Now we have instant communication and continuous information transferral.

And paradoxically this amazing technology often results in fragmentation, and alienation from each other.

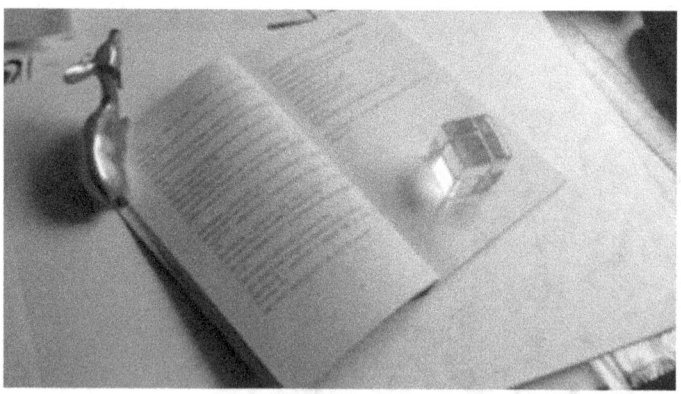

122. money

123. multi-phonic *Rabelaisdada*

Yesterday I went to see the *Bells from The Deep* show at the Hundred Years Gallery in Hoxton.

The musician Graham Mackeachan (who organizes the music programmes at the Gallery) told me about an event which they'd held on the 31st January, during which they set up a network of tubes on both floors of the gallery, through which they projected live readings of various texts, including extracts from *Rabelaisdada*, read by the artist Jill Rock. The musicians Saul Eisenberg and Giles Leaman performed with their Junk Orchestra – a multi-sonic and multi-text performance, with the children also enjoying taking part, as could be seen from the photographs of the event.

Bells From the Deep was named after Werner Herzog's film about Russian mysticism, and the works on display are strikingly virtuosic, from Neville Sattentau's paintings in vivid tempera colours inspired by medieval illuminated manuscripts and Persian miniatures, to Gianluca Bonomo's breathtaking image of a flock of camera-headed birds flying towards you, realised in ballpoint pen, though looking as if precisely engraved.

124. iridescent mind

The iridescent mind leaps from one area to another and yet maintains focus.

125. light and sound

Everything became softly amorphous, as if the china of the plate flowed and the steel of the knife were liquid. Meanwhile the concussion of the waves breaking fell with muffled thuds, like logs falling, on the shore.

126. audiovisual montage

Sound/image synaesthesia is the key to audiovisual montage.

Sometimes the music anticipates a change of shot, sometimes the music responds to a change of shot.

On occasion, shot change and sound are totally simultaneous.

The flow of the music and the film interact so that there is not too much sameness of pace, they play off each other, as well as join each other.

The rhythms of the film act in dynamic counterpoint to the rhythms in the music.

It's like when you flick a disc-shaped stone.

Spinning, it bounces off the surfaces of the water several times, rapidly moving forwards in leaps.

What happens here is an interweaving of images and music, which has its own unity in combination, leaping forwards.

I try other start-points for the music in relation to the film.

After experimenting for several hours, I return finally to my first choice: the audiovisual zero point.

This is the unique point at which sound/music and image combine in the most effective way, out of all the possible combinations.

So many combinations are possible that the unconscious mind has to find the correct combination. If you try to use your conscious mind to find the zero point, I don't think you'll find it. Either side of this zero point won't do: the result will either grate or be tedious.

This is because the music/film combination should not only fit at certain points of the work, but it should fit throughout, like water in a plant.

They are very different, but they fit.

127. *Rabelaisdada,* a satire

Dante, Cervantes, Shakespeare, Goethe - these artists of the word have all transcended the boundaries of their original culture and language. Yet there is a writer who has also achieved a similar level of international recognition, but remains an illustrious unknown: François Rabelais.

I came to him via James Joyce, but I didn't have time to read him during the relentless examinations period (from age 14 to 22). The opportunity came much later: after composing the operas *The Kingdom*, *The Cathars*, and *Empedocles*, I wanted to work on something which would make me laugh.

I spent a year reading all of Rabelais' five books, in his original 16th century French. Then I had great fun translating, and re-creating for a libretto, the parts I had chosen, nearly all of them from *The Fourth Book* and *The Fifth Book*, which tend to be overlooked in English.

When I had finished the libretto I was stuck, I couldn't find any space for the music. Then I realised that the music had already introduced itself into the fabric of the work: it was there, in the words. When *Rabelaisdada* was performed, the actors had the text in front of them on music stands, and they were dressed formally, like classical musicians.

The mix of different kinds of language in this work brought to mind the satirical Dada language experiments and performances. Marcel Duchamp said that 'Rabelais is Dada', so it was thought that *Rabelaidada* would be a good name for this Rabelais re-invention.

It is a work in a modulable form: it can be performed, or read as an illustrated book, or both. The latter happened when the Long-Eared Birds episode was performed with the audience taking part, at the Hundred Years Gallery, as part of the artist Jill Rock's WHITEOUT Festival.

The Fourth Book and *The Fifth Book* by Rabelais are about a search, by a group of characters, for the Oracle of the Holy Bottle. We have already met two of these personalities in previous books: Pantagruel and Panurge. There is also Brother Lardoon (Frère Jehan des Entonneurs in the original text), and I added Alcofrybas Nasier, much in the way Renaissance painters added themselves to their work, hidden away in a crowd in their larger canvasses. Alcofrybas Nasier is an anagram of his own name used by Rabelais as a protective pen-name for his first books *Gargantua* and *Pantagruel*.

Rabelais is probably in all of his characters. In non-satirical novels it's not always clear whether the characters the novelists create actually represent what their author feels or believes. Take *In Cold Blood* by Truman Capote. Here the novelist presents a detailed background to a deeply disturbing local news story, and he does it in a passionless almost anonymous, journalistically photographic way. It is different with satirical novels: the use of humour, with its distancing effect, obscures the fact that satirists inevitably present much of themselves in their work, one of the reasons they tend to get into trouble. The characters the authors create in satire don't need the believable psychological complexities of characters in 'straight' novels. They bear more of the author's ideas - their complexities reside in the concepts they represent, which are the satirist's ideas. Psychological naturalism has usually no useful function for an author who has specific targets to hit.

Satire has an indirect element to it. Rabelais uses humour as a prism, re-directing his flow of thought into greater complexity than is possible with a direct ray of attack. The result of this complexity and indirect manner means that the satirist's targets are not always immediately aware that they have been hit. But when they *do* become aware, their counter-attack is all the more vicious. By then it's too late - everyone else has already understood what is happening.

But one could say that the main enemy of satire is obscurity. Some of Rabelais' writings are totally obscure today: we just don't know to whom or to what he was referring. The comic resonance disappears; his text becomes like a foreign language we don't know, though paradoxically we understand the meaning of each word. This is why, in a part of *Rabelaisdada* I left blank spaces at various points in a story, so that the actor who plays the part of the storyteller can refer to an issue of local interest, then, at another point a national problem can be mentioned, then lastly any international issue currently dominating the news can be referred to. All of these will be of interest or of concern to the audience at the time of the performance. This technique will ensure that this story in *Rabelaisdada* will always be up-to-date and comprehensible to a contemporary audience. Therefore these news items, local, national and international, will remain a valid target for satire, anywhere this play is performed.

However I encountered this problem of obscurity again, when I was faced with Rabelais' description of the Isle of Contrivance. This is an uninhabited island with a mysterious vegetation consisting of tools which hang from trees and grow up from the ground. To gain some meaning from Rabelais' long lists of implements, I decided to translate his descriptions into the language of line. I used the ball-point pen's sharp unambiguous line to evoke the strange clarity of the Isle of Contrivance as seen by Panurge and his companions from the deck of the Thalamegius. In 1994 in Moscow, a Russian friend told me 'This is like Russia today' when she saw these drawings.

The end of *Rabelaisdada* is perhaps more mysterious. I didn't like the description of the Oracle of the Holy Bottle in *The Fifth Book*. The Oracle seemed to me to be a little artificial amidst its palatial surroundings. Some think that Rabelais didn't write this part at all - the style here certainly lacks his satirical edge and natural exuberance.

In rethinking the Oracle I collected local newspapers from different countries and cut out those sharp and lucid drawings of consumer products that one used to find in the classified ads section at the back. I then anthropomorphised a drawing of a very large bottle and filled it with these drawings of consumer products. This became my Oracle of the Holy Bottle, and I had the Thalamegius sail towards it.

I had a problem finishing *Rabelaisdada*, as Panurge, Pantagruel and the others just wouldn't shut up. So I disemvowelled them: I took away their vowels. This is the mysterious effect the Oracle has on those who venture near it. Perhaps it happens so that the Oracle can make its oracular disembottled pronouncement in awesome silence: DRINK!

Then as the Oracle's head fades, we see the Thalamegius emerge from it. Then the Thalamegius itself gradually disappears into the white of the last page.

Why the Thalamegius disappears the way it does, I don't know - that's just the way it happened. Was it because drawings and texts both consist of lines? That may be part of an answer.

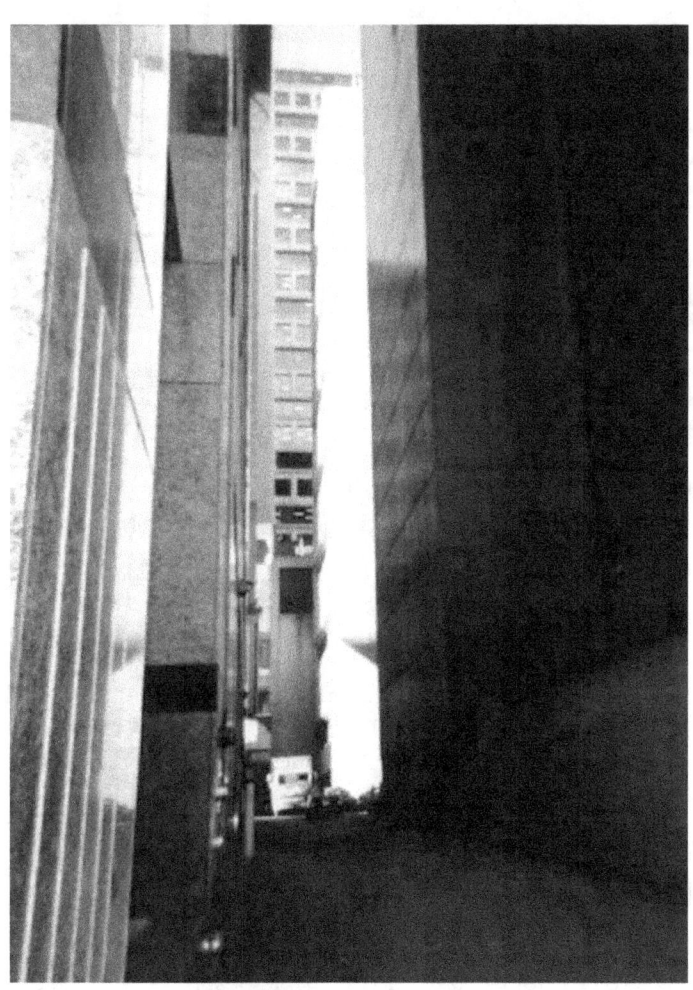

128. an American space

129. making places

Early morning sun on early spring trees outside the bedroom window.

Sunlit trees against blue sky.

Sunlit trees against grey sky.

Trees in shadow against grey sky.

Trees in shadow against blue sky.

How do you make your places?

You can live your whole life somewhere in a city and never go down one particular street, or one particular part of that city.

This unknown region, small or big, isn't part of you and you are not part of it.

In our lives we *are* the places we inhabit.

And because of daily interactions and the stress these can cause, the places we inhabit can gradually become invisible through habit and dislike – we become blind to their treasures –

for example, a lone seagull quietly unnoticed, looking at the world from the very top of a mast on a high domed tower.

Places we dislike we avoid, so they don't become a corrosive part of us – we are just not open to their possible beauty.

People and other creatures make a place, and they form a continuum of being.

Where becomes part of what one *is*.

Where you have been and what you do there become part of what you are.

How you *deal* with place and places becomes part of you in evolution -

create your own places and make yourself evolve -

without being oppressive.

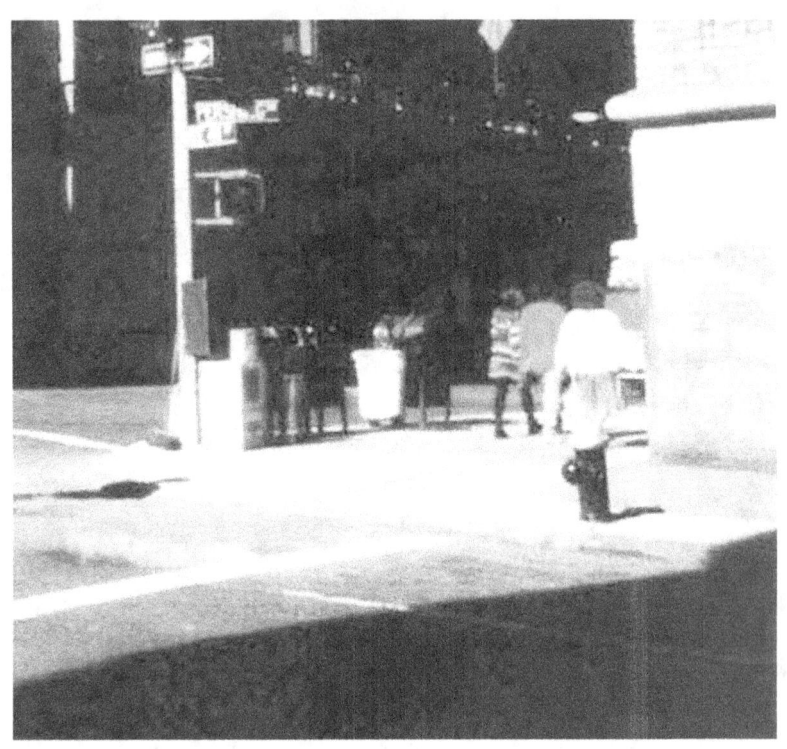

130. Manhattan morning

origins

Non-attributed texts and photographs are mine, as are all the headings.

2. **arty**

    Do you say that someone is 'musicy'? I've never heard anyone described as being musicy.

    I like Ad Reinhardt's paintings, and his writings on art, and this statement was inspired by his writings.

4. **rhythm**

    This is why, in the digital visual world, the fight should be against the dominance of bilateral symmetry.

    For example see/hear *Edge of Chaos*:

    https://www.youtube.com/watch?v=8PepxZHKk-4

5. **when it's useful to be unknown**

    This experience happened when I was setting up a Greek Poetry Archive for an American publisher, which was later purchased by another international publisher.

    Two of the volumes in the Greek Poetry Archive featured the poetry, writings and collages by Odysseus Elytis: *The Oxopetra Elegies* (1996) and *Carte Blanche* (1999), both translated by David Connolly.

    Odysseus Elytis (1911-1996) won the Nobel Prize for Literature in 1979. Elytis corresponded with Lawrence Durrell, and Albert Camus, who also appear elsewhere in this book.

Strangely, companies can now buy the past.

For example: you buy a publisher, and you can become the actual publisher of their books from the past – you published books which appeared years *before* you even thought of buying that publishing company.

This means that when you were working *for* a publisher, actually in the future it turns out that you weren't, as your work will be for that future company you would never have thought at that time that you would be (or have been) working for…

A new 'future is the past' tense needs to be devised for such a situation. It brings to mind the Soviet Russian joke:

'the future is certain, but the past is unpredictable' –

except that here the future is as unpredictable as the past, as there is no difference between past and future: the past has been transformed into a phantom that has never existed, and so it becomes as unforeseeable as the future.

6. archival connections

My first opera *The Kingdom* was directed by Rufus Collins (formerly of The Living Theatre) and co-directed by Henk Tjon.

The Kingdom was first performed in 1984, at the Engelenbak Theatre in the centre of Amsterdam.

A former warehouse for sugar imported from the Caribbean, this theatre was most suitable for an opera about the Haitian Revolution.

The audience was seated on three sides of the stage, and so they were present as if they were participants in each scene.

This theatrical setting was ideal: the last thing I wanted was the distance from the performance space which audiences experience in traditional opera houses.

In addition, the 35 performers attended over sixty rehearsals and workshops, to be ready to perform the various dance styles in the opera, and the various styles of choral music, which are also vital in this work.

Nowhere was heard the vibrato-laden voice I intentionally avoided in this opera (and in my two subsequent operas).

Instead, the singing was all clearly in tune, as were the voices in the choruses, united in harmony, not all wobbling muddily at different levels of vibrato, as in traditional opera choruses.

There was no orchestra to separate the performers from the audience, as the music was part of the action: the musicians performed on the stage, as in Kabuki theatre. The large-scale orchestral sections were realised electro-acoustically, and were projected into the theatre.

Rufus Collins (1935 -1996) was an African-American theatre director and actor.

Henk Tjon (1948 - 2009) was a Surinamese theatre director and playwright.

They founded the music, theatre and dance company DNA, from the first production of *The Kingdom*.

In the introduction to his novel *The Kingdom of This World*, Carpentier presented his influential concept of 'magic realism'.

http://www.ocatilloaudiovisual.com/the-kingdom.html

7. Manhattan morning

See also 91 and 130.

8. Empedocles in Oxford

http://www.ocatilloaudiovisual.com/empedocles.html

11. *River*, from *Diversions*

Diversions is a music/film in which the pre-digital past and the digital present/future are intertwined.

I composed the orchestral score in the late Seventies, inspired by my first impressions of London at that time, and the paintings of Jasper Johns, Motherwell and De Kooning.

In 2017 I shot and edited the digital film, and made a digital realization of the orchestral score. Visually in *Diversions* you see the London of 2017, in an audiovisual counterpoint with music I composed in the pre-digital past.

A key theme in *Diversions* is the interaction of the city with nature, an interaction that remains very evident in London.

12. art in the present

'Picasso Speaks,' *The Arts*, New York, May 1923, pp. 315-26.

13. legislators

Primo Levi, *The Mirror Maker*, trans. Raymond Rosenthal, Methuen London, 1990, p.111.

15. a leap, a dip

from *The Waves*, by Virginia Woolf.

18. American Abstract Expressionists

Machines, River, Cityzens was the original order of the three movement orchestral piece, which became *Diversions* in its music/film version, around forty years later, with the revised order: *Machines, Cityzens, River*. For more about *Diversions*, see note 11, above.

19. Joyeux party!

A still from the music/film *Oserake and The River That Walks*. *Diary of a Music/Film*, about the realisation of this audiovisual work, can be found in *Cinema and the Audiovisual Imagination*, pp 177-231.

21. Havana morning

This photograph also appears in *I'm Back*, a film I made of sixteen poems by Spike Hawkins, which he performs, rather than just reading them. These poems were recorded by Steve Dracup at his Audio-Surgery studio.

https://www.youtube.com/watch?v=Ki7hXs9PaB0

22. failed pictures

The first statement is by Picasso, from Jaime Sabartés, *Picasso, An Intimate Portrait*, 1948, p. 209.

For Picasso's comment on a 'finished' canvas, see *Picasso on Art*, Dore Ashton, 1972, p.31.

23. theorism

Claudette Robertson, 2017.

24. spatial/temporal orientation

Kandinsky's letter to Albers is on page 50 in *Josef Albers and Wassily Kandinsky: Friends in Exile – A Decade of Correspondence, 1929-1940*, Hudson Hills Press, Manchester, Vermont, 2010.

The correct position of Albers' woodcut *Opera* can be seen on page 59 in the above book.

25. glass mask

This image, and the image in No 1, also appear in the music/film *River*, from *Diversions* (2017).

26. *Breaking the Frame*

Documentary filmmaker Professor Marielle Nitoslawska was my supervisor for my master's film (*Oserake and The River That Walks*) at the Mel Hoppenheim School of Cinema, Montreal. Her film production classes were an inspiration, an excellent example when I went on to teach filmmaking.

Her colleague, the experimental filmmaker Professor Richard Kerr, introduced me to the Stan Brakhage Archive at the film school, a rich source of ideas and experiences from an American artist who struggled in an initially unforgiving environment.

Brakhage gave a talk and introduced us to his *Dante Quartet* (1987), as part of a festival of his work, just a year before he died in 2003.

28. ***Working from Ignorance*** (2001)

> The Mel Hoppenheim School of Cinema in Montreal is unusual in that it is linked to an art school, the Faculty of Fine Arts: both are part of Concordia University. This means that filmmakers are given an unusual opportunity to interact with visual artists, including artist filmmakers. I wrote *Working from Ignorance* (and *Ways of Knowing*, No 117, below) for Professor Lon Dubinsky's course: Art: Ideas and Practices (2000-2001).
>
> What I found particularly refreshing about his classes, was that they were open and totally free of mind-limiting academic jargon. We were encouraged to share our influences and ideas, and to talk freely about developments in contemporary art.
>
> I have made minor revisions in both texts, but *Working from Ignorance* and *Ways of Knowing* both retain for me a strong sense of their origins in the creative atmosphere of Lon Dubinsky's classes, and they remain a source of new areas of thought and practice that I'm still exploring today.

29. **a unique gallery**

> http://hundredyearsgallery.co.uk/about/
>
> http://www.ocatilloaudiovisual.com/musicfilms.html

36. **prize**

> This text was influenced by the jocular tone of some of the poems by Arp, the Dada artist and poet, whose work has influenced my music for many years, and continues to do so.

37. **Montreal snow**

> Still from the music/film *Oserake and The River That Walks*.

38. not illustrations

Picasso. Gilot/Lake, *Life with Picasso*, 1990, p. 325.

42. The kye-nee-ma

The quote from J.J. Thompson is from *With Eisenstein in Hollywood*, by Ivor Montagu, p. 32.

Eisenstein's description of Kapitsa explaining his research to him at the Mond Laboratory, Cambridge, can be found in his *Immoral Memories*, p. 165.

44. time and memory

Wolfgang Pauli, from *Atom and Archetype: the Pauli/Jung Letters, 1932-1958*, p. 29.

45. immigration

Still from the music/film *Oserake and The River That Walks*.

47. I am

Marina Tsvetaeva, from her poem *Homesickness*, translated by Helen Szamuely.

50. a secret

Bertrand Russell, *The Conquest of Happiness*.

51. door of the spirits

For more doors of the spirits:

https://caribbeanantillean.weebly.com/doors-of-the-spirits.html

52. what everyone likes

Federico Fellini, in *I, Fellini*, Charlotte Chandler and Federico Fellini, Cooper Square Press, 2001, p. 223.

55. aspects of education

Both statements are from Zhuangzi.

Translation from ancient Chinese texts is a real challenge.

The first statement is a translation from the original Chinese text, by Michael Dufresne.

The second statement is a simplification of the same text, found on the Net.

The original is from Chapter 13 (*The Way of Heaven*).

Zhuangzi is also known as Chuang-Tzu.

Many thanks to Michael Dufresne for his translation, and for finding the source of this text for me. In the Philosophy Department at the University of Hawaii at Manoa, he is working on comparative philosophy, including Chinese philosophy.

His article 'The illusion of teaching and learning: Zhuangzi, Wittgenstein, and the groundlessness of language' is published in the international journal *Educational Philosophy and Theory*, Vol 49, Issue 12: The Cultivation of Self in East Asian Philosophy of Education.

59. collective opinion

Wolfgang Pauli, from *Atom and Archetype: the Pauli/Jung Letters, 1932-1958*, p.31.

60. a story from World War I

Robert Le Ricolais, my maternal grandfather, served with the Chasseurs Alpins in World War I.

He was awarded the Croix de Guerre, and the Médaille Militaire. My mother and I found these medals when clearing out the cupboard in his studio in Paris, after his death. There was also a rifle bullet, and a card he'd sent to his mother, written in pencil. He thanks her for the cake she'd sent, which he'd shared with his fellow soldiers. He also tells her that during the previous night there was so much shelling that it was like daylight.

62. intellectuals

Frank Lloyd Wright, interviewed by Mike Wallace, 1957.

63. melting into air – a letter from my grandfather

Robert Le Ricolais (1894-1977), architect and structural engineer.

1935 Medal of Distinction (Society of French Civil Engineers) for his Isoflex system.

1953 Started work at the Department of Architecture, the Graduate School of Fine Arts, the University of Pennsylvania

1962 Grand Prix de l'Architecture of the Cercle d'Etudes Architecturales.
Awarding the prize, André Malraux described him as
'the father of space structures'.
The prize itself was very appropriate, due to the influence of crystal structures on his work: it was a huge clear quartz crystal, the size of a wine bottle. I wonder where it is now?.

1965 Retrospective exhibition at the Palais de la Découverte in the Grand Palais, Paris.

The influence of space structures devised by Le Ricolais can be seen in various buildings and structures today, for example in London.

These influences can be traced to structures described and photographed in 'Things themselves are lying, and so are their images', in *Structures Implicit and Explicit*, Graduate School of Fine Arts, University of Pennsylvania, 1973, pages 81-109:

(1) the 'Gherkin' building, London: The FPR system (Funicular Polygon of Revolution), pages 94, 95.

(2) the Millenium Dome, London - domes derived from structures found in radiolaria:
'From the point of view of the radiolarian, the geodesic dome is three hundred million years old', pages 89-91.

(3) the Wembley Stadium 'ropes', London: Tension Net tubes, pages 96, 97.

(4) the Millenium Bridge, London: the Polyten bridge, pages 108, 109.
Initially there were problems of stability with this bridge. As can be seen, the original structural model by Le Ricolais doesn't appear to have been followed accurately.

The Spanish/Swiss architect Santiago Caltrava is one of the few architects who has publicly acknowledged the influence of Le Ricolais.

See also the issue on Le Ricolais: *Le Carré bleu*, No 2, 1994.

66. ice on hotel, Montreal

Still from the music/film *Oserake and The River That Walks*.

69. open/close

The first line is by Albert Camus, in *La postérité du soleil* : texts by Camus, photographs by Henriette Grindat, presented by the poet René Char.

The four-line fragment is by Empedocles.

I use it to start the third and last act of my dance opera.

This final act from *Empedocles* features the four deaths of the philosopher: by earth, by water, by air, by fire.

72. frontiers

From Robert Le Ricolais: *Matières*, with photographs by Henriette Grindat, in *Structures Implicit and Explicit*, Graduate School of Fine Arts, University of Pennsylvania, 1973, p.11.

The Swiss photographer Henriette Grindat was fascinated by the effects of light in coastal towns and landscapes.

In the book *La postérité du soleil*, she collaborated with the writer Albert Camus and the poet René Char, bringing together their texts and her photographs.

Her partner, the artist Albert Yersin was a friend of my grandfather.

73. night trees

This image was inspired by Gogol's description of trees lit at night, in his novel *Dead Souls*.

I was introduced to this novel by Glenn, an elderly American composer, who looked a little like a pilgrim father, with his long white beard.

I met Glenn at an SPNM Festival. The SPNM (Society for the Promotion of New Music) was called by some composers the Society for the Prevention of New Music.

Much of the music at this festival lived up to the latter description: feeble 'me-too' imitations of pieces by Stockhausen and Boulez, and the dull and faintly comical acts of influence between people competing with each other in a very narrow environment.

Glenn and I were bored by all this, but in conversation, his mention of Gogol's novel *Dead Souls* opens a vast new vista, a great gift for me. This new perspective led to me writing a libretto based on *Dead Souls*, called *Chichikov*, named after Gogol's anti-hero in his novel.

Chichikov was performed as a play with masks, at the Cockpit Theatre in London, in 1981.

I never solved the problem of composing the music for what would have been a comic opera, as timing in comedy changes with each performance: it is unpredictable to a greater extent than most timing is in music, which is why music is generally absent (or just suggested, as a form of musical punctuation) for comic exchanges in comic operas.

Two sketches for *Chichikov*.

http://www.ocatilloaudiovisual.com/earlier.html

76. the artist as enemy

Orson Welles, interviewed by Huw Wheldon in 1960, after *The Magnificent Ambersons* (1942) and *A Touch of Evil* (1958).

77. no style

Picasso. From André Verdet, *Picasso et ses environs*, in *Entretiens, notes et écrits sur la peinture: Braque, Léger, Matisse, Picasso. Paris 1978*, p.199.

79. chaos

Still from *Cityzens*, the second movement of my music/film *Diversions in Three Movements* (2017).

86. vertical/horizontal

The first text is based on Albert Camus' comment on the photograph of an ancient well, taken by the photographer Henriette Grindat.

It's from *La postérité du soleil* : a sequence of thirty texts by Albert Camus, which face thirty photographs by Henriette Grindat, (1952).

The second text, by Robert Le Ricolais, also deals with an unexpected progression from a horizontal perspective towards a perspective in depth. It accompanies a photograph by Grindat, of scattered thin strands of seaweed emerging from a white surface of sand.

From *Matières*, six texts by Le Ricolais, which are combined with six photographs by Henriette Grindat (1964).
It's in *Structures Implicit and Explicit*, The Graduate School of Fine Arts, University of Pennsylvania, 1973, p.122.

87. the crocodile and the hen

This story about the crocodile and the hen is from the *Anthologie nègre*, pages 221-222. This is a 400-page anthology of African stories, poems, songs and legends from countries and peoples throughout the African continent, assembled by the French writer Blaise Cendrars, and first published in 1921.

The translation of the story is mine, and I've adapted it slightly, in the traditional manner of storytellers.

88. America

This happened in July 1981.

89. *The Virginity of Place* (2000)

This is an essay I wrote for the filmmaker Jean-Pierre Lefebvre, in his film class at Concordia University, in 2000.

His films are independently produced, without reference to commercial cinema. His open mind and his curiosity about everything were very refreshing, and I found that his classes were a democratic delight - they were relaxed and most enjoyable.

I learned much from them, including a way to teach cinema.

The documentary about Pasolini, *Whoever Tells the Truth Must Die* (1981) was made by the Dutch director Philo Bregstein.

91. Manhattan Morning

Also see 7 above, and 130 below.

95. Cap-Haïtien, 14th August

This is an extract from *Haitian Summer*, a book about my six-week research trip in Haïti, in 1981, for *The Kingdom*.

Once I'd realized that the local middle-class were hopeless as a source of information, I was given a lot of help by local people, especially in Cap-Haïtien, a key location in the historical period which features in my opera *The Kingdom*.

I was very lucky to be invited by the master-drummer Michel Ciryac to a re-creation of the historical Cérémonie du Bois Caïman, on the night of the 14th to the 15th August, which takes place each year, and which features in Alejo Carpentier's novel *The Kingdom of This World*.

This book is an account of the Haïtian Revolution, on which I based the opera's libretto. The Cérémonie du Bois Caïman is re-created in the second act of the opera, which shows the revolt against the French colonists, led by the Jamaican, Boukman.

During one of the rehearsals for this scene in Amsterdam, a Dutch member of the cast went into a trance. Fortunately the Co-Director Henk Tjon had experience of the traditional Maroon ceremonies in Suriname, and so he was able to deal with this unexpected situation. He directed the Cérémonie du Bois Caïman scene in the second act of the opera.

Notre-Dame Frappez!, the song that is sung on the night of the 14th August, is a reference to the feisty spirit Erzulie Dantor, from the Pétro rite. She is at the same time Notre-Dame, and so she is associated both with the Assumption of the Virgin Mary on the 15th August, and the Cérémonie du Bois Caïman.

Like the opera *The Kingdom*, this is an example of cultural hybridisation, which remains a source of fascination for me, and it appears in all aspects of my work.

The end of this extract from *Haitian Summer* leads to the Temple Nago, for the first part of the re-creation of the Cérémonie du Bois Caïman:

https://caribbeanantillean.weebly.com/haitian-summer.html

This research trip to Haïti for *The Kingdom* led me to use this approach for the other two operas:
a trip to the Cathar sites in South-West France for *The Cathars*, and a trip to Sicily to visit the sites associated with the philosopher Empedocles, for the dance opera *Empedocles*.

And in the music/films, locations and music are even more closely brought together.

97. monstrous things

Robert Le Ricolais, *Matières*, with photographs by Henriette Grindat, in *Structures Implicit and Explicit*, Graduate School of Fine Arts, University of Pennsylvania, 1973, p.116.

98. work-table, Montreal

Still from the music/film *Oserake and The River That Walks*. (On the table is my score for the music for this music/film).

99. non-linear narratives

[1] Quentin Bell, *Virginia Woolf: A Biography*, Vol. II: *Mrs Woolf, 1912-1941*, Hogarth Press, London, 1972.

[2] *A Writer's Diary: Being Extracts from the Diary of Virginia Woolf*, ed. Leonard Woolf, Hogarth Press, London, 1953.

[3] The French painter Jacques Raverat discussed the nature of writing, in correspondence with Virginia Woolf.

From *The Novels of Virginia Woolf*, by Hermione Lee, Methuen & Co. Ltd., 1977.

100. chance

Arp, *Jours effeuillés*, NRF, Gallimard, 1966, p. 420.

102. inspiring Hockney retrospective

[1] Thanks to the artist filmmaker Dennis Dracup who reminded me of this.
(I believe that multiple styles are a feature that is often found in the best and most enduring music).

[2] From the illuminating BBC4 documentary, *The Silk Road*, presented by Dr Sam Willis.

104. a village near St Petersburg

Seen from the Moscow to St Petersburg train, when foreigners were permitted to travel on day trains.

108. waiting

Still from *Machines*, the first movement of the music/film *Diversions* (2017), first shown at the Hundred Years Gallery, on the 21st December 2017.

113. the Jarman Building

This was a wonderful opportunity to develop an exploration of the audiovisual, mostly based on my book *Cinema and the Audiovisual Imagination*. I showed Spike Lee's *Do the Right Thing*, Kubrick's *2001, A Space Odyssey*, David Lynch's *Lost Highway*, Kurosawa's *Throne of Blood*, and Pasolini's *Gospel According to Matthew*.

And there was a lot of material for the seminars:
Chris Marker's *La jetée*, extracts from Dreyer's *Passion of Joan of Arc*, Herzog's *Heart of Glass*, with his hypnotised actors; some extracts from Eisenstein, including the Coronation Scene from *Ivan the Terrible*, with another form of hypnotic acting.

I also had the chance to show Paradjanov's *Legend of the Surami Fortress* (this great director's work is so rarely seen in the UK), a section of Sokurov's *Mother and Son*, extracts from Tarkovsky's *The Sacrifice*, and Kaneto Shindo's *Onibaba*.

Herzog's documentary on the Antarctic, *Encounters at the End of the World* was also a hit with the students.

I finished with Derek Jarman's very moving last film, *Blue*. It worked perfectly on the large screen in the lecture theatre with an excellent sound system, the ideal work to end a course on the audiovisual.

114. perfection

Sergei Eisenstein, *Immoral Memories, An autobiography*, trans. Herbert Marshall, 1985, p. 237.

116. foreign

Frank Lloyd Wright, in *Frank Lloyd Wright on Architecture, Nature, and the Human Spirit*, ed. Bruce Brooks Pfeiffer, p. 65.

117. *Ways of Knowing* (2000)

See No 28, above.

118. *Diversions*

The quote from Primo Levi is from Ann Goldstein's introduction to *A Tranquil Star* (p.16), a collection of texts by Primo Levi, translated into English by Ann Goldstein and Alessandra Bastagli, published in 2007.

119. illusions of illusions

Le Ricolais mentions this Chinese proverb in his introduction to *Matières*, a set of photographs by Henriette Grindat, published in counterpoint with his texts. I tried to trace the proverb, but without success.

122. money

Pages 6 and 7 from *Rabelaisdada*, the book version of my opera libretto. On the recommendation of the musicologist Professor Richard Langham Smith, the libretto was performed as a play at the Institut Français in London in 1993, by the Paines Plough Theatre Company, directed by Anna Furse.

The two pages feature three simultaneous bargainings, in three different (invented) languages: only the amounts of money mentioned can be understood.

https://rabelaisdada.weebly.com

125. light and sound

Virginia Woolf, *The Waves*.

127. *Rabelaisdada,* **a satire**

This is a revised version of a talk I gave at a conference at the Université de Paris III, Sorbonne Nouvelle, in 1998.

129. My thanks to Claudette for the key three-word conclusion.

130. Manhattan morning

This is the third in a sequence of three images: see 7 and 91 above.

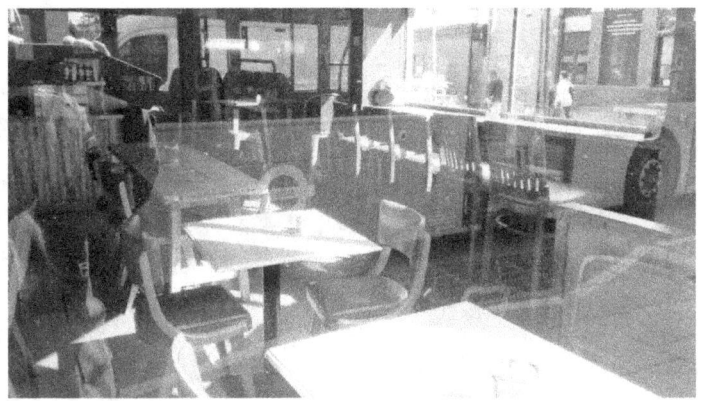

131. reflections

All images in the book are black and white, to bring them closer to the texts.

131 is an Eisenstein prime.

www.ingramcontent.com/pod-product-compliance
Lightning Source LLC
Chambersburg PA
CBHW071053240526
45471CB00015B/1788